# MEL BAY'S COMPLETE BALALAIKA BOOK

## By Bibs Ekkel

A COMPREHENSIVE GUIDE & TUTOR

INCLUDES INFORMATION ON ALL ORCHESTRAL SIZES OF BALALAIKA AND DOMRA

### CD CONTENTS

| Track | Contents | Track | Contents | Track | Contents | Track | Contents |
|---|---|---|---|---|---|---|---|
| 1 | Ex. 1 [0:13] | 25 | Ex. 25 [0:10] | 50 | Ex. 50 [0:42] | 75 | Ex. 75 [0:07] |
| 2 | Ex. 2 [0:13] | 26 | Ex. 26 [0:17] | 51 | Ex. 51 [0:05] | 76 | Ex. 76 [0:58] |
| 3 | Ex. 3 [0:14] | 27 | Ex. 27 [0:11] | 52 | Ex. 52 [0:08] | 77 | Ex. 77 [0:18] |
| 4 | Ex. 4 [0:17] | 28 | Ex. 28 [0:38] | 53 | Ex. 53 [0:07] | 78 | Ex. 78 [0:06] |
| 5 | Ex. 5 [0:18] | 29 | Ex. 29 [0:07] | 54 | Ex. 54 [0:06] | 79 | Ex. 79 [0:30] |
| 6 | Ex. 6 [0:41] | 30 | Ex. 30 [0:18] | 55 | Ex. 55 [0:05] | 80 | Ex. 80 [0:09] |
| 7 | Ex. 7 [0:15] | 31 | Ex. 31 [0:09] | 56 | Ex. 56 [0:06] | 80 | Ex. 81 [0:10] |
| 8 | Ex. 8 [0:14] | 32 | Ex. 32 [0:08] | 57 | Ex. 57 [0:05] | 82 | Ex. 82 [0:06] |
| 9 | Ex. 9 [0:18] | 33 | Ex. 33 [0:35] | 58 | Ex. 58 [0:08] | 83 | Ex. 83 [0:15] |
| 10 | Ex. 10 [1:23] | 34 | Ex. 34 [0:14] | 59 | Ex. 60 [0:09] | 84 | Ex. 84 [0:07] |
| 11 | Ex. 11 & 12 [0:51] | 35 | Ex. 35 [0:48] | 60 | Ex. 61 [0:07] | 85 | Ex. 85 [0:08] |
| 12 | Ex. 13 [0:34] | 36 | Ex. 36 [0:17] | 61 | Ex. 62 [0:06] | 86 | Ex. 86 [0:08] |
| 13 | "Korobushka," The Pedlar's Box [0:46] | 37 | Ex. 37 [0:58] | 62 | Waltz Durand No. 1 [0:16] | 87 | Ex. 87 [0:14] |
| | | 38 | Ex. 38 [0:21] | 63 | Ex. 63 [0:06] | 88 | Ex. 88 [0:40] |
| 14 | Ex. 14 & 15 [1:22] | 39 | Ex. 39 [0:48] | 64 | Ex. 64 [0:05] | 89 | Ex. 89 [0:15] |
| 15 | Tam na Bloniu [0:42] | 40 | Ex. 40 [0:28] | 65 | Ex. 65 [0:09] | 90 | Ex. 90 [0:20] |
| 16 | Ex. 16 [0:16] | 41 | Ex. 41 [0:11] | 66 | Ex. 66 [0:08] | 91 | Ex. 91 [0:19] |
| 17 | Ex. 17 [1:35] | 42 | Ex. 42 [0:08] | 67 | Ex. 67 [0:10] | 92 | Ex. 92 [0:05] |
| 18 | Ex. 18 [0:46] | 43 | Ex. 43 [0:42] | 68 | Ex. 68 & "I Went Up A Hill" [0:39] | 93 | Ex. 93 [0:12] |
| 19 | Ex. 19 [0:09] | 44 | Ex. 44 [0:13] | 69 | Ex. 69 [0:02] | 94 | Ex. 94 [0:21] |
| 20 | Ex. 20 [0:25] | 45 | Ex. 45 [0:19] | 70 | Ex. 70 [0:06] | 95 | Ex. 95 [012] |
| 21 | Ex. 21 [0:21] | 46 | Ex. 46 [0:11] | 71 | Ex. 71 [0:11] | 96 | Ex. 96 & 97 [0:38] |
| 22 | Ex. 22 [0:07] | 47 | Ex. 47 [0:25] | 72 | Ex. 72 [0:35] | 97 | Ex. 98 [0:29] |
| 23 | Ex. 23 [0:09] | 48 | Ex. 48 [0:10] | 73 | Ex. 73 [0:28] | 98 | Ex. 99, Parts 1 & 2 [1:22] |
| 24 | Ex. 24 [0:07] | 49 | Ex. 49 [0:09] | 74 | Ex. 74 [0:18] | 99 | Daily Exercises [1:50] |



*Visit us on the Web at http://www.melbay.com —*
*E-mail us at email@melbay.com*

1 2 3 4 5 6 7 8 9 0

# About the balalaika...

For many the balalaika, with its extreme moods of gaiety and sadness, is seen as a reflection of the Russian character. No one is quite sure just when this instrument with its distinctive shape and sound first appeared, but it has always been inexorably bound to Russian folklore. By the turn of the century, the balalaika had developed from primitive roots into the modern concert instrument that today is held in high regard in Russia. It is used in performances of classical, modern, and [of course] folk music and taught in schools and conservatoires throughout the country. Of the five sizes of orchestral balalaikas, only the prima is capable of performing as a solo instrument. Its three strings (tuned A E E) are strummed or plucked with the fingers, not a plectrum, making it a difficult instrument to master. This fact, combined with the lack of adequate learning material for the instrument, may explain why – unlike the mandolin, banjo and guitar – the balalaika has remained largely confined to its native country. Hopefully this book will go some way towards correcting this situation and in some small degree help this truly unique and astoundingly beautiful instrument attain the international popularity it so richly deserves.

# And the author...

Born in London, U.K., of mixed Polish-English background, Bibs Ekkel is one of few outstanding exponents of the balalaika outside Russia. His career as a professional balalaika player has covered concerts, cabaret, recordings, films, and innumerable radio and TV appearances throughout Europe and North America. It has earned him recognition too in the balalaika's Motherland, where he has performed on radio and TV as well as at Moscow's prestigious "Hall of Columns" and "Tchaikovsky Hall." He has lectured on Russian folk music at American Universities, coauthored a BBC radio educational series on the subject and worked as Russian music adviser for several BBC TV productions. He has also had Russian and Polish speaking roles in a variety of movies. In addition to his activities as soloist, Bibs Ekkel runs a highly successful Russian music and dance ensemble, "Tziganka" (which has toured internationally since 1975), an instrumental quartet "Balalaika Potpourri" (started by him in Vancouver in 1989, soon after his move there from London), and the duo "Russian Tornado" (specifically aimed at school concerts). Some of his many recordings have been issued by "Russkiy Disk" Moscow, CBS Israel, and "Decca" in London.

*The author welcomes questions or comments relating to the material in this tutor.*

***Written: 1982***
***First printed edition (Fully revised and enlarged) Autumn 1995***

## *Acknowledgments*

*...thanks to:*

my **mother** for transforming my original manuscript into legible print at the typewriter;

my friend, guitarist **Rick Sharpe,** for taking the photos;

flamboyant **Ciro** at his Pizza Pomodoro in London, where I sat writing the tutor each night with generous amounts of "Peroni" during my breaks from the gig down the road;

**Francie Fyte** in Washington D.C. for all her time and effort with the word-processor;

both the late **Misha Danilov**, Director of the Folk Music Faculty at St. Petersburg Conservatoire and **Margarita Bischoff** in Tucson for their helpful comments...

*...but most importantly to:*

my dear wife **Lara**, for her countless patient hours, days, and weeks spent either at the computer or with paste and scissors in hand, loyally seeing my idealistic goal through to the end and creating order out of my inspired muddle.

*To my children:*

***Slavek, Ruslan, Shiny (Miroslav), Alyoshka and Ludmila***

***- and to all those not afraid to march to a different drumbeat.***

Ясно, что при широкомъ распространенiи въ народныхъ массахъ кружковъ и оркестровъ, -возможность существованiя и развитiя которыхъ нынѣ уже доказана, - такое развлеченiе является однимъ изъ самыхъ могучихъ рычаговъ къ утвержденiю трезвости. Давъ народу оздоравливающую и доступную ему духовную пищу, легче будетъ бороться и съ водкой, -этимъ повальнымъ зломъ нашей деревни.....

В. Л. - „В. В. Андреевъ и его Великорусскiй Оркестръ“
С.-Петербургъ 1909

. . . there is a certain blind street player who, having added to the normally two-stringed balalaika another differently tuned string, plays not only arias, minuets, and Polish dances, but also whole works through allegro, andante and presto with exceptional artistry. . .

Yakob Shtelin
"Music and Ballet in 18th Century Russia" (1760)

# Table of Contents

# Foreword

Like some poor relative, the balalaika is all too often left out of encyclopedias and musical dictionaries and, when included, often dismissed as a "primitive, guitar-like instrument of limited range found in Eastern Europe". Such descriptions do no justice to this unique and very beautiful instrument that can, in the hands of a master, produce a range of sound and wealth of expression unrivalled by any other instrument.

One of the greatest problems directly affecting the balalaika's popularity is its almost total confinement to Russia and the non-availability in the West of literature, music, and teachers for the instrument. The purpose of this book is not only to provide the student with a precise description of all the various techniques available to the balalaika player, but also to contradict misconceptions about the instrument and how it is played.

(Unfortunately, the lack of balalaika playing traditions and material in the West has led to the publication of some scurrilously inaccurate teaching methods. One widely available book, notwithstanding its superlative-sounding title, has, to the author's personal knowledge, caused more than one budding student to give up learning the instrument altogether.)

The playing methods described and illustrated here conform to standards as taught in Russia today and include minor additions and innovations stemming from the author's own practical experience. As with other instruments, disagreement exists as to certain playing techniques on the balalaika. Russia being the vast country it is, there are geographical differences in accepted playing norms. Passages can usually be played in more than one way and in different styles. Many players, becoming adept at certain styles over the years, find it difficult to accept alternatives to their own preferred style of playing: recognizing their own as being the only correct one. As every hand is slightly different both in shape and size, it is only natural that variations will occur between each hand's comfortable playing position.

One should always remember the immortal guitarist, Django Rheinhardt, who, with two fingers of his left hand missing, necessarily broke countless rules. He not only proved that devotion and determination come first on the list of requirements for becoming an able musician, but showed up many other musicians in the process.

The author has endeavoured wherever possible to indicate where acceptable variations in method and style may occur. However, certain contentious issues should be cleared up straight away.

## Balalaikas with six strings

Long ago most balalaikas were homemade, and the shape of the body, the materials used, and the number of strings (two or three being the most common) varied greatly. In time three strings became established as the norm.

Today six-stringed balalaikas (3 double strings) are quite common among cheaper models (not only the German and Romanian imports, but also those produced by some Russian instrument factories, especially the one in Rostov which supplies most of the Ukraine). At the turn of the century four-stringed prima balalaikas (with a double top string) were not uncommon. In today's Russia, possibly due to a new atmosphere of innovation and departure from rigid socialist convention, we are seeing some orchestras experimenting with four-string alto and contrabass balalaikas.

While a double-strung balalaika makes a perfectly adequate instrument for strumming a simple accompaniment to singing (or maybe for playing with a plectrum as a balalaika-shaped mandolin), to be properly played the **prima** balalaika should have but **three** strings.

One of the most important features of the balalaika is the wealth of different sounds that can be produced on it using the various techniques described in this book. Most of these are possible only on an instrument with single strings. Double strings dampen the volume and slow the fingers down, making complicated strokes impossible and limiting the scope of the player.

*Double strings are usually a sign of a poor instrument.*

## Playing the balalaika standing up

*Only when correctly seated can the player make full use of the balalaika's many playing techniques.*

Some players *do* play standing up, mainly for visual effect or to stroll around tables in a restaurant (no doubt improving the tips greatly). However, playing is greatly hindered by the instrument not being held steady to allow both hands the necessary freedom of movement – something which no amount of neck-slings or straps can compensate for.

## Playing the balalaika with a plectrum/pick

*The proper way to play the prima balalaika is with the fingers only.*

As Russian folk instruments developed and improved, it became traditional for the balalaika to be played with the finger and its sister-instrument, the domra, with a plectrum. Sometimes people use a plectrum, either as a means to bluff the playing of the instrument, or to be able to play louder without getting sore fingers (especially in noisy playing situations where no amplification is available). However, it could be argued that playing the balalaika with a plectrum is akin to playing the mandolin with the fingers, a thimble, or the edge of a book; that's just not the way it is done. The hallmark of the *balalaika sound* is its soft quality due to the strings being strummed or plucked by the skin - in contrast to the harsher sound produced by a pick or by the nails.

## Playing a balalaika with all steel strings

The last 100 years have seen the prima balalaika lifted from its lowly status as a primitive accompanying instrument to that of a solo instrument in its own right. In establishing a school of playing technique and a vast literature for the balalaika, several generations of professional balalaika players have accepted that the prima sounds best with one steel string and two of nylon or gut. (With the development in recent years of acoustically superior nylon strings, gut has fallen out of use.) Although cheap instruments are almost invariably sold with all-steel strings, these give a somewhat tinny sound. Nylon strings soften and improve the instrument's tone and, furthermore, when all strings are being played at once, allow the melody line on the top string to stand out.

## Finding the right strings

There are few commercially produced balalaika strings available in the West, and those that are tend to be – almost invariably – the wrong gauge. Some years ago Cathedral, a British company, brought some out - but they were far too thin. Individually-sold Russian steel (A) strings, if you can get them, are cheap and of the correct gauge, but usually of poor quality steel.

*Short of making one's own strings, it is best to find steel banjo strings (as these have a loop end) of between 11 and 12 thou' - thousandths of an inch - (0.28 - 0.3mm) in thickness. I personally prefer 11.5 thou' strings, although these can be hard to find.*

The sets of balalaika strings sold in Russian shops consist, for some reason, of three steel strings. Although steel 2nd and 3rd strings and the jangly sound they produce are sometimes preferred by Russian villagers, who mostly use the instrument for simple accompaniment to singing, solo playing requires one steel and two nylon strings.

Russian players, in the absence of a source of high quality acoustic nylon strings, often make do with nylon fishing line of the appropriate thickness. Inevitably, theories among musicians abound as to the best brand of fishing line to use. At the moment, Japanese fishing line is most sought-after. It could be said that the fishing line has done for the balalaika what the wire coat hanger has done for car radios.

*For the E-strings one should use good quality nylon guitar thirds (G's). I would personally recommend La Bella "Golden" or "Black" if you can find them. These seem to be the strings generally preferred by players in Russia.*

## Tuning & Bridge Position

The steel top string (on the right when facing the instrument) is tuned to A. The other two strings, the second and third, are tuned lower and to the same note - middle E. Before tuning the strings, the correct position of the bridge must be found. There are several ways to check this:

- When pressed down at the twelfth fret, each string should sound an octave above the open (unpressed) string.
- Pressing the A-string at the 7th fret should give E an octave above the E of the open 2nd and 3rd strings.
- The harmonic (see section on harmonics) obtained at the 12th fret should be of the same pitch as the note produced when *pressing* the same string at the 12th fret. (Once the player has mastered harmonics, this will be the simplest way to check for the correct position of the bridge.)
- If you have problems, you can use eyes instead of ears: take a tape measure. Check that the 12th fret is exactly half way between the nut and bridge.

*Moving the bridge towards the neck of the instrument (thereby shortening the string length), will raise the note.*

Once the bridge is in the correct position, the top string should be tuned to A using a piano or tuning fork. Pressing the 2nd and 3rd strings at the 5th fret should also give A.

(Although AEE has become the accepted standard tuning for the prima balalaika, this was by no means always the case. Even today certain Russian villagers are to be found using a variety of alternative traditional tunings. See section: "Brief History of the Balalaika," p. 92.)

## Bridge

The bridge is free-moving (not stuck down) and is made of hardwood – usually ebony, rosewood or maple (sycamore). The material, size, and shape of the bridge all have a bearing on the tone and are individual matters for each instrument. Sometimes bridges may be made of different woods glued together. One should experiment with variously shaped bridges made of different types of wood to find the one producing the best sound for a particular instrument. This usually entails having a collection of different bridges made or, better still, making them oneself.

The bottom of the bridge must fit snugly onto the soundboard at all points and care should be taken to check this thoroughly. (Does the bridge move about; can you see daylight under the bridge; can you slide a piece of paper under any part of the bridge?) If the bridge doesn't fit tightly, the sound will suffer and the bridge may creak or move out of position during playing. Players often solve this last problem by depositing a thin layer of rosin (as used on violin bows) on the bottom of the bridge to prevent movement. This can be done by heating the bottom of the bridge gently over a flame before wiping it quickly over the rosin to coat it with a thin layer. Alternately, one can wrap a small piece of rosin in newspaper, thoroughly crush it, and then dab the sticky powder onto the soundboard or the bottom of the bridge.

The height of the bridge also has a bearing on the sound: the higher it is, the louder. However, the main consideration here is to achieve a comfortable string height for playing. Very often certain adjustments have to be made to a new instrument, including lowering the height of the strings at the bridge or nut to make playing easier.

The middle string is usually moved over slightly towards the 3rd string to facilitate pizzicato playing on the top and middle string.

Recommended string heights and distances are provided in the String Adjustment Chart below.

**RECOMMENDED ADJUSTMENT OF STRINGS IN MM**[1]

*Distance between strings at:*

| | | | | |
|---|---|---|---|---|
| *Nut* | - | 1st and 2nd | - | 10-11mm |
| | | 2nd and 3rd | - | 10-11mm |
| *Bridge* | - | 1st and 2nd | - | 24-26mm |
| | | 2nd and 3rd | - | 14-15mm |

*Height of strings above:*

| | | |
|---|---|---|
| 1st fret | - | 0.6-0.8mm |
| 12th fret | - | 3-3.2mm |

## Fingerboard

The number of frets on a balalaika may vary from 17 to 31. Early improved instruments commonly had 17 or 19 frets. Today, good instruments invariably have at least 24 (providing two octaves on the top string) with 27 being ideal.

The scratchplate may be inlaid or raised (overhanging the soundboard). It is made of smooth hardwood and serves to protect the vulnerable soft pine or spruce soundboard from scratches the right hand may produce during playing and also keeps any right hand noise to a minimum.

Plastic or mother-of-pearl dots or shapes adorn the fingerboard to act as a visual guide for the left hand.

[1] See *OSNOVY IGRY NA BALALAIKE (The Basics of Balalaika Playing)* by Prof. A. Shalov – Muzyka, Leningrad, 1970.

## General Advice

- All of the fingernails should be kept short so they do not interfere with playing. This applies in particular to the right index finger, the fleshy fingertip of which is used for most of the playing. If the left-hand fingernails grow too long, they will prevent the fingers from pressing down perpendicularly on the string to produce a clean sound. If the nail of the R.H. "playing" index finger is not kept trimmed down, it will make contact with the string, spoiling the sound and possibly breaking or splitting sideways, thus making playing painful.

- The strings should be kept clean. In particular, the steel string must be wiped free of moisture after playing or it may rust and act like a saw on the fingers.

- The balalaika is best kept in a hard case and protected from extreme temperatures and humidity.

*It should be possible for a musical person to learn to play the balalaika without learning to read music. Learning melodies by ear and using this tutor for explanation of the techniques used should do the trick. For such people, the cipher system used in the first part of the tutor may be useful: it entails mastering only the principles of timing and learning the value of notes as written. For this purpose a section on timing is provided at the back of the tutor section.*

The student is strongly advised to learn to read music. Without sufficient space in this tutor to adequately explain the principles of musical notation, those totally unfamiliar with music theory should get themselves an appropriate book on the subject. Meanwhile, apart from the aforementioned brief "Introduction to Timing", this tutor explains musical signs and terms in the course of its lessons only where it is relevant to some particular aspect of balalaika technique. A "Glossary of Musical Signs" at the back of the book contains concise explanations of the signs likely to be encountered.

# Tuning of Orchestral Instruments

*The true tunings of all the various balalaikas and domras both common and less common in use today are given below.*

*The **prima balalaika** is the solo instrument among balalaikas and unquestionably the most difficult to master. It is the one for which this tutor was written.*

## Present day Tunings of Balalaikas and Domras

| BALALAIKA<br>Strings = 3, 2, 1 | DOMRA - 3 String<br>Strings = 3, 2, 1 | DOMRA - 4 String<br>Strings = 3, 2, 1 |
|---|---|---|
| **Piccolo**<br>(rarely used, music notated an octave lower)<br>B E A | **Piccolo**<br>(notated an octave lower)<br>B E A | **Piccolo**<br>C G D A |
| **Prima**<br>E E A | **Prima**<br>E A D | **Prima**<br>G D A E |
| **Secundo**<br>A A D | **Mezzo-Soprano**<br>(rarely used)<br>B E A | |
| **Alto**<br>(notated an octave higher in treble clef)<br>E E A | **Alto**<br>(notated an octave higher in treble clef)<br>E A D | **Alto**<br>C G D A |
| | **Tenor**<br>(notated an octave higher in treble clef)<br>B E A | **Tenor**<br>(notated an octave higher in treble clef)<br>G D A E |
| **Bass**<br>E A D | **Bass**<br>E A D | **Bass**<br>C G D A |
| **Contrabass**<br>(notated an octave higher)<br>E A D | **Contrabass**<br>(rarely used, notated an octave higher)<br>E A D<br>or<br>A D G | **Contrabass**<br>(notated an octave higher)<br>E A D G |

# STRINGS FOR THE BALALAIKA ORCHESTRA - SPECIFICATIONS

## Balalaika

| Size (L = distance nut to bridge) | String # | Tuned | Total Length (mm) | Frequency (Hz) | Diameter (mm) | | Tension (Kg) | Pressure (Kg/mm²) |
|---|---|---|---|---|---|---|---|---|
| | | | | | Core | Winding | | |
| **Prima**<br>(L = 435 mm) | 1<br>2 - 3 | *$a_1$*<br>*$e_1$ - $e_1$* | 700<br>720 | 440<br>329.6 | 0.25 - 0.30<br>0.35 - 0.40 | -<br>- | 8.3<br>8.3 | 117<br>81 |
| **Secunda**<br>(L = 475 mm) | 1<br>2 - 3 | *$d_1$*<br>*a - a* | 730<br>790 | 293.6<br>220 | 0.30<br>0.35 | 0.12<br>0.18 | 11.9<br>13.5 | 169<br>140 |
| **Alto**<br>(L = 535 mm) | 1<br>2 - 3 | *a*<br>*e - e* | 790<br>840 | 220<br>164.8 | 0.30<br>0.35 | 0.17<br>0.26 | 13<br>13.4 | 184<br>139.5 |
| **Bass**<br>(L = 700 mm) | 1<br>2<br>3 | *d*<br>*A*<br>*E* | 1110<br>1150<br>1180 | 146.8<br>110<br>82.4 | 0.40<br>0.40<br>0.50 | 0.22<br>0.40<br>0.60 | 21.5<br>23<br>23.5 | 171<br>183<br>120 |
| **Contrabass**<br>(L = 1100mm) | 1<br>2<br>3 | *D*<br>*$A_1$*<br>*$E_1$* | 1580<br>1640<br>1660 | 73.4<br>55<br>41.2 | 0.50<br>0.60<br>0.70 | 0.5<br>0.70<br>0.95 | 33.3<br>31.5<br>31.3 | 170<br>111<br>81.5 |

## Domra - (3 string)

| Size (L = distance nut to bridge) | String # | Tuned | Total Length (mm) | Frequency (Hz) | Diameter (mm) | | Tension (Kg) | Pressure (Kg/mm²) |
|---|---|---|---|---|---|---|---|---|
| | | | | | Core | Winding | | |
| **Piccolo**<br>(L = 283 mm) | 1<br>2<br>3 | *$a_2$*<br>*$e_2$*<br>*$b_1$* | 450<br>490<br>510 | 880<br>659.2<br>493.84 | 0.25<br>0.35<br>0.30 | -<br>-<br>0.10 | 9.8<br>10.7<br>11.4 | 200<br>111<br>161.5 |
| **Prima**<br>(L = 400 mm) | 1<br>2<br>3 | *$d_2$*<br>*$a_1$*<br>*$e_1$* | 600<br>640<br>670 | 587.2<br>440<br>329.6 | 0.30<br>0.40<br>0.30 | -<br>-<br>0.13 | 12.5<br>12.5<br>12.6 | 177<br>100<br>178 |
| **Alto**<br>(L = 500 mm) | 1<br>2<br>3 | *$d_1$*<br>*a*<br>*e* | 750<br>780<br>810 | 299.6<br>220<br>164.8 | 0.35<br>0.35<br>0.35 | 0.10<br>0.20<br>0.35 | 15.6<br>15.9<br>16.9 | 162<br>165.5<br>176 |
| **Tenor**<br>(L = 585 mm) | 1<br>2<br>3 | *a*<br>*e*<br>*B* | 850<br>890<br>920 | 220<br>164.8<br>123.46 | 0.40<br>0.40<br>0.50 | 0.15<br>0.28<br>0.50 | 19.0<br>19.5<br>26.6 | 151<br>155<br>135 |
| **Bass**<br>(L = 715 mm) | 1<br>2<br>3 | *d*<br>*A*<br>*E* | 1020<br>1090<br>1110 | 146.8<br>110<br>82.4 | 0.40<br>0.40<br>0.50 | 0.24<br>0.40<br>0.60 | 19.4<br>17.6<br>22.6 | 154<br>140<br>114 |

## Domra - (4 string)

| Size (L = distance nut to bridge) | String # | Tuned | Total Length (mm) | Frequency (Hz) | Diameter (mm) | | Tension (Kg) | Pressure (Kg/mm²) |
|---|---|---|---|---|---|---|---|---|
| | | | | | Core | Winding | | |
| **Piccolo** (L = 274 mm) | 1 | $a_2$ | 500 | 880 | 0.25 | - | 9.2 | 187 |
| | 2 | $d_2$ | 500 | 587.2 | 0.30 | - | 10.6 | 84.5 |
| | 3 | $g_1$ | 500 | 391.92 | 0.40 | 0.17 | 10.8 | 152 |
| | 4 | $c_1$ | 500 | 291.6 | | 0.24 | 11.3 | 90 |
| **Prima** (L = 350 mm) | 1 | $e_2$ | 630 | 659.2 | 0.30 | - | 12.1 | 171 |
| | 2 | $a_1$ | 630 | 440.0 | 0.40 | - | 9.6 | 76 |
| | 3 | $d_1$ | 630 | 293.6 | 0.35 | 0.17 | 11.6 | 120 |
| | 4 | $g$ | 630 | 195.96 | 0.40 | 0.35 | 13.0 | 103.5 |
| **Alto** (L = 420 mm) | 1 | $a_1$ | 730 | 440.0 | 0.40 | - | 13.8 | 110 |
| | 2 | $d_1$ | 730 | 293.6 | 0.35 | 0.17 | 16.7 | 174 |
| | 3 | $g$ | 730 | 195.96 | 0.50 | 0.35 | 22.2 | 113 |
| | 4 | $c$ | 730 | 130.8 | 0.60 | 0.60 | 22.1 | 78 |
| **Tenor** (L = 475mm) | 1 | $e_1$ | 800 | 329.6 | 0.35 | 0.11 | 18.5 | 192 |
| | 2 | $a$ | 800 | 220.0 | 0.35 | 0.24 | 17.2 | 179 |
| | 3 | $d$ | 800 | 146.8 | 0.60 | 0.40 | 21.8 | 77 |
| | 4 | $G$ | 800 | 97.98 | 0.60 | 0.60 | 15.9 | 50 |
| **Bass** (L = 630 mm) | 1 | $a$ | 960 | 220.0 | 0.35 | 0.17 | 21.2 | 220 |
| | 2 | $d$ | 960 | 146.8 | 0.50 | 0.28 | 22.1 | 113 |
| | 3 | $G$ | 960 | 97.98 | 0.50 | 0.60 | 24.8 | 126 |
| | 4 | $C$ | 960 | 65.4 | 0.60 | 0.80 | 18.5 | 65.5 |
| **Contrabass** (L = 990 mm) | 1 | $G$ | 1560 | 97.98 | 0.50 | 0.28 | 24.1 | 122.5 |
| | 2 | $D$ | 1560 | 73.4 | 0.60 | 0.70 | 48 | 170 |
| | 3 | $A_1$ | 1560 | 55.0 | 0.70 | 0.90 | 42 | 109 |
| | 4 | $E_1$ | 1560 | 41.2 | 1.0 | 1.2 | 46.5 | 59 |

# Picks For Orchestral Instruments

**Balalaikas** The *Piccolo* balalaika has today been supplanted by the piccolo domra, but when used is similarly played with a hard (tortoiseshell, plastic, or equivalent) pick[1].

*Secundo* and *Alto* are played either with the fingers or a small soft leather pick.

The *Bass* and *Contrabass* are played with proportionally larger leather picks.

**Domras** All domras are played with a pick, usually a hard one (tortioseshell or the equivalent) for treble or alto instruments, and a soft leather one for the bass and contrabass.

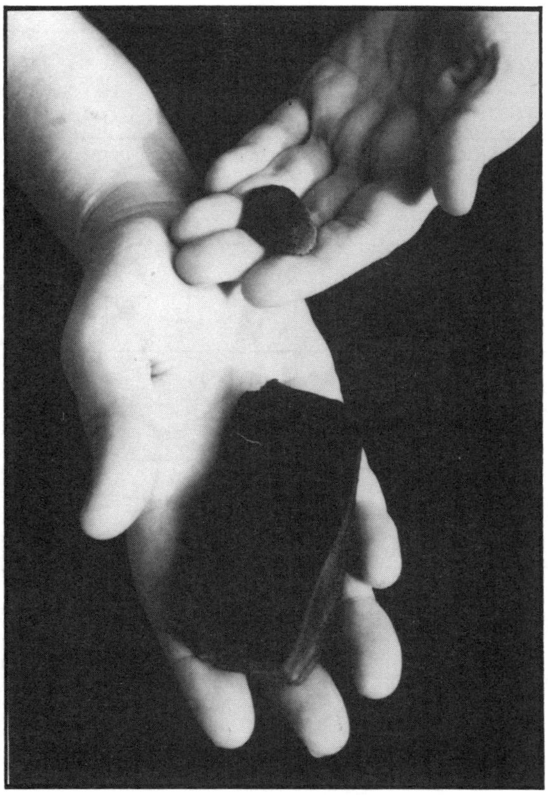

## Making the pick

The ideal pick needs to be home-made, as shops do not sell picks of the correct shape, size, thickness, and type of materials. Although some players have settled for polyethylene[2] (this having a soft, less "clicky" quality than tortoiseshell) leather is preferred by most Russian players for the bass instruments. Musicians carefully consider each newly marketed modern polymer for possible canditature as plectrum material; the search for the ideal pick is far from over!

Thick stiff shoe sole leather is used (single-ply for the alto, possibly three-ply for the contrabass). The pick is cut and sanded to shape, played a little "in the raw" to check for comfort, then soaked in castor oil for two weeks to make it supple.

*Photo: Alto and Contrabass leather picks*

---

[1] Mass production of the piccolo balalaika at Leningrad's Lunacharsky Instrument Factory, the largest in the USSR, officially ceased in 1932.

[2] In the Moscow Radio and TV Orchestra (now called: Ostankino), domra players switch to polyethylene picks for close-miked recording sessions.

# Chord Shapes for Prima (and Alto) Balalaika

**MAJOR**

| | | | | | | |
|---|---|---|---|---|---|---|
| **C** | 3<br>0<br>3 | 7<br>8<br>3 | 10<br>12<br>8 | 15<br>15<br>12 | | |
| **C♯**<br>**D♭** | 4<br>4<br>1 | 8<br>9<br>4 | 11<br>13<br>9 | 16<br>16<br>13 | | |
| **D** | 5<br>5<br>2 | 0<br>2<br>2 | 5<br>5<br>5 | 9<br>10<br>5 | 12<br>14<br>10 | 17<br>17<br>14 |
| **D♯**<br>**E♭** | 6<br>6<br>3 | 1<br>3<br>3 | 6<br>6<br>6 | 10<br>11<br>6 | 13<br>15<br>11 | |
| **E** | 2<br>0<br>4 | 7<br>7<br>4 | 11<br>12<br>7 | 14<br>16<br>12 | | |
| **F** | 3<br>5<br>1 | 3<br>5<br>5 | 3<br>1<br>1 | 8<br>8<br>5 | 12<br>13<br>8 | 15<br>17<br>13 |
| **F♯**<br>**G♭** | 4<br>6<br>2 | 1<br>2<br>2 | 4<br>2<br>2 | 4<br>6<br>6 | 9<br>9<br>6 | 13<br>14<br>9 |
| **G** | 5<br>7<br>3 | 2<br>3<br>3 | 5<br>3<br>3 | 10<br>10<br>7 | 14<br>15<br>10 | |
| **G♯**<br>**A♭** | 6<br>8<br>4 | 3<br>4<br>4 | 6<br>4<br>4 | 6<br>8<br>8 | 11<br>11<br>18 | 15<br>16<br>11 |
| **A** | 4<br>0<br>5 | 7<br>9<br>5 | 12<br>12<br>9 | 16<br>17<br>12 | | |
| **A♯**<br>**B♭** | 5<br>6<br>1 | 1<br>1<br>1 | 5<br>6<br>6 | 8<br>10<br>6 | 13<br>13<br>10 | |
| **B** | 6<br>7<br>2 | 2<br>2<br>2 | 6<br>7<br>7 | 9<br>11<br>7 | 14<br>14<br>11 | |

**MINOR**

| | | | | | | | |
|---|---|---|---|---|---|---|---|
| **Cm** | 6<br>8<br>3 | 3<br>3<br>3 | 6<br>3<br>3 | 6<br>8<br>8 | 10<br>11<br>8 | 15<br>15<br>11 | |
| **C♯m**<br>**D♭m** | 4<br>0<br>4 | 7<br>9<br>4 | 11<br>12<br>9 | 16<br>16<br>12 | | | |
| **Dm** | 5<br>5<br>1 | 5<br>5<br>5 | 0<br>1<br>1 | 8<br>10<br>5 | 12<br>13<br>10 | 17<br>17<br>13 | |
| **D♯m**<br>**E♭m** | 6<br>6<br>2 | 6<br>6<br>6 | 1<br>2<br>2 | 9<br>11<br>6 | 13<br>14<br>11 | | |
| **Em** | 2<br>0<br>3 | 7<br>7<br>4 | 10<br>12<br>7 | 14<br>15<br>12 | | | |
| **Fm** | 3<br>4<br>1 | 3<br>1<br>1 | 3<br>4<br>4 | 8<br>8<br>4 | 11<br>13<br>8 | 15<br>16<br>13 | |
| **F♯m**<br>**G♭m** | 4<br>5<br>2 | 0<br>2<br>2 | 4<br>2<br>2 | 4<br>5<br>5 | 9<br>9<br>5 | 12<br>14<br>9 | 16<br>17<br>14 |
| **Gm** | 5<br>6<br>3 | 1<br>3<br>3 | 5<br>3<br>3 | 5<br>6<br>6 | 10<br>10<br>6 | 13<br>15<br>10 | 17<br>18<br>15 |
| **G♯m**<br>**A♭m** | 6<br>7<br>4 | 2<br>4<br>4 | 6<br>4<br>4 | 6<br>7<br>7 | 11<br>11<br>7 | 14<br>16<br>11 | |
| **Am** | 3<br>0<br>5 | 7<br>8<br>5 | 12<br>12<br>8 | 15<br>17<br>12 | | | |
| **A♯m**<br>**B♭m** | 4<br>6<br>1 | 1<br>1<br>1 | 4<br>1<br>1 | 4<br>6<br>6 | 8<br>9<br>6 | 13<br>13<br>9 | |
| **Bm** | 5<br>7<br>2 | 2<br>2<br>2 | 5<br>2<br>2 | 5<br>7<br>7 | 9<br>10<br>7 | 14<br>14<br>10 | |

| **C°**<br>**E♭°**<br>**F♯°**<br>**A°** | **Diminished** | | | |
|---|---|---|---|---|
| | 3<br>5<br>2 | 6<br>8<br>5 | 9<br>11<br>8 | 12<br>14<br>11 |

| **C♯°**<br>**E°**<br>**G°**<br>**B♭°** | **Diminished** | | | |
|---|---|---|---|---|
| | 1<br>3<br>0 | 4<br>6<br>3 | 7<br>9<br>6 | 10<br>12<br>9 |

| **B°**<br>**D°**<br>**F°**<br>**G♯°** | **Diminished** | | | |
|---|---|---|---|---|
| | 2<br>4<br>1 | 5<br>7<br>4 | 8<br>10<br>7 | 11<br>13<br>10 |

| SEVENTHS | | | | | | | | |
|---|---|---|---|---|---|---|---|---|
| $C^7$ | **3** | 3 | 1 | 7 | 7 | | | |
| | **3** | 6 | 3 | 8 | 6 | | | |
| | **3** | 3 | 0 | 6 | 3 | | | |
| $C\sharp^7$ / $D\flat^7$ | 2 | 4 | 8 | 8 | | | | |
| | 4 | 7 | 9 | 7 | | | | |
| | 1 | 4 | 7 | 4 | | | | |
| $D^7$ | 3 | 5 | 9 | 9 | | | | |
| | 5 | 8 | 10 | 8 | | | | |
| | 2 | 5 | 8 | 5 | | | | |
| $D\sharp^7$ / $E\flat^7$ | 4 | 6 | 10 | 10 | | | | |
| | 6 | 9 | 11 | 9 | | | | |
| | 3 | 6 | 9 | 6 | | | | |
| $E^7$ | 5 | 5 | 7 | 11 | 11 | | | |
| | 0 | 7 | 10 | 12 | 10 | | | |
| | 4 | 4 | 7 | 10 | 7 | | | |
| $F^7$ | 6 | 6 | 8 | 12 | | | | |
| | 5 | 8 | 11 | 11 | | | | |
| | 1 | 5 | 8 | 8 | | | | |
| $F\sharp^7$ / $G\flat^7$ | 1 | 4 | 7 | 7 | 9 | | | |
| | 2 | 6 | 9 | 6 | 12 | | | |
| | 0 | 0 | 6 | 2 | 9 | | | |
| $G^7$ | 2 | 5 | 8 | 8 | 10 | | | |
| | 3 | 7 | 10 | 7 | 13 | | | |
| | 1 | 1 | 7 | 3 | 10 | | | |
| $G\sharp^7$ / $A\flat^7$ | 3 | 9 | 9 | 11 | | | | |
| | 4 | 11 | 8 | 14 | | | | |
| | 2 | 8 | 4 | 11 | | | | |
| $A^7$ | 4 | 0 | 4 | 10 | 10 | 12 | | |
| | 0 | 3 | 5 | 12 | 9 | 15 | | |
| | 3 | 0 | 3 | 9 | 5 | 12 | | |
| $A\sharp^7$ / $B\flat^7$ | 1 | 5 | 5 | 11 | 11 | 13 | | |
| | 4 | 4 | 6 | 13 | 10 | 15 | | |
| | 1 | 1 | 4 | 10 | 6 | 13 | | |
| $B^7$ | 2 | 6 | **6** | **6** | 6 | 12 | 12 | 14 |
| | 5 | 5 | **5** | **7** | 7 | 11 | 14 | 17 |
| | 2 | 2 | **5** | **7** | 5 | 7 | 11 | 14 |

| MINOR SIXTHS | | | | | | | | |
|---|---|---|---|---|---|---|---|---|
| $Cm^6$ | **0** | 3 | 6 | 6 | 12 | | | |
| | **3** | 5 | 5 | 8 | 11 | | | |
| | **3** | 3 | 3 | 5 | 8 | | | |
| $C\sharp m^6$ | 1 | 4 | 4 | 7 | 7 | 13 | | |
| | 4 | 6 | 6 | 6 | 9 | 12 | | |
| | 0 | 4 | 0 | 4 | 6 | 9 | | |
| $Dm^6$ | 2 | **2** | **2** | 5 | 5 | 8 | 8 | 14 |
| | 5 | **1** | **5** | 7 | 7 | 7 | 10 | 13 |
| | 1 | **1** | **5** | 5 | 1 | 5 | 7 | 10 |
| $D\sharp m^6$ / $E\flat m^6$ | 3 | 6 | 6 | 9 | 9 | 15 | | |
| | 6 | 8 | 8 | 8 | 11 | 14 | | |
| | 2 | 6 | 2 | 6 | 8 | 11 | | |
| $Em^6$ | 4 | 4 | 7 | 7 | 10 | 10 | 16 | |
| | 0 | 7 | 9 | 9 | 9 | 12 | 15 | |
| | 3 | 3 | 7 | 3 | 7 | 9 | 12 | |
| $Fm^6$ | 5 | **5** | 5 | 8 | 8 | 11 | 11 | |
| | 4 | **4** | 8 | 10 | 10 | 10 | 13 | |
| | 1 | **4** | 4 | 8 | 4 | 8 | 10 | |
| $F\sharp m^6$ | 6 | 6 | 9 | 9 | 12 | 12 | | |
| | 5 | 9 | 11 | 11 | 11 | 14 | | |
| | 2 | 5 | 9 | 5 | 9 | 11 | | |
| $Gm^6$ | 7 | 1 | 5 | 7 | 10 | 10 | 13 | 13 |
| | 6 | 0 | 0 | 10 | 13 | 12 | 12 | 15 |
| | 3 | 3 | 6 | 6 | 10 | 6 | 10 | 12 |
| $G\sharp m^6$ | 2 | 8 | 8 | 11 | 11 | 14 | 14 | |
| | 4 | 7 | 11 | 13 | 13 | 13 | 16 | |
| | 1 | 4 | 7 | 11 | 7 | 11 | 13 | |
| $Am^6$ | 3 | 0 | 0 | 3 | 9 | 9 | 12 | 15 |
| | 0 | 0 | 2 | 5 | 8 | 12 | 14 | 14 |
| | 2 | 2 | 0 | 2 | 5 | 8 | 12 | 12 |
| $B\flat m^6$ | 4 | 1 | 4 | 10 | 10 | 13 | 16 | |
| | 3 | 3 | 6 | 9 | 13 | 15 | 15 | |
| | 1 | 1 | 3 | 6 | 9 | 13 | 13 | |
| $Bm^6$ | 5 | 2 | 5 | 11 | 11 | 11 | 14 | |
| | 4 | 4 | 7 | 10 | 12 | 14 | 16 | |
| | 2 | 2 | 4 | 7 | 10 | 10 | 14 | |

• Notes played on the 2nd and 3rd strings are interchangeable:

eg: Am = 3 / 0 / 5 or 3 / 5 / 0

| | | | |
|---|---|---|---|
| | 3 | | 3 |
| eg: Am = | 0 | or | 5 |
| | 5 | | 0 |

• Simplified 2 note chords are highlighted.

# Prima Balalaika

## Various Bridge Shapes

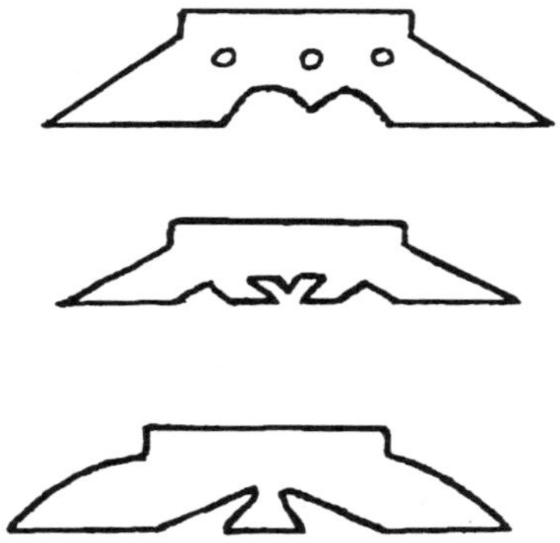

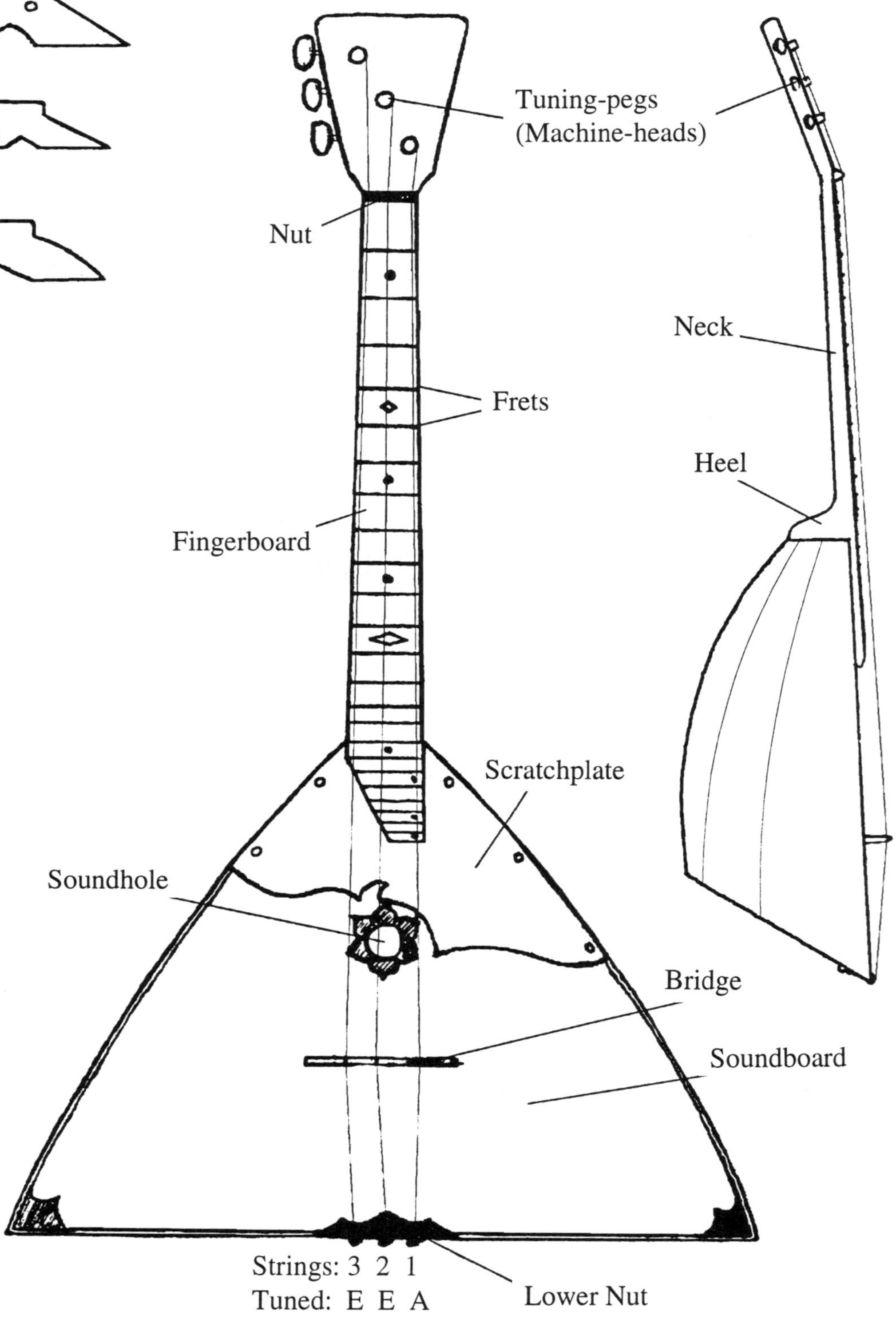

# Tutor Section

# STRINGS

Regardless of what strings may have been on the balalaika when it was acquired, the following ones are recommended and are the accepted norm in Russia today.

***First String*** *(on the right when facing the instrument)*

- steel loop-end between 11 and 12 thou' (0.28 - 0.3mm) thickness

***Second & Third Strings***

- nylon guitar thirds (Gs) (see foreword for recommendations)

# TUNING

The first string is tuned to A

Both the second and third string are tuned to E (i.e. both to the same note).

Pressing down both nylon E-strings at the 5th fret (as shown) should give the same note as the open top string.

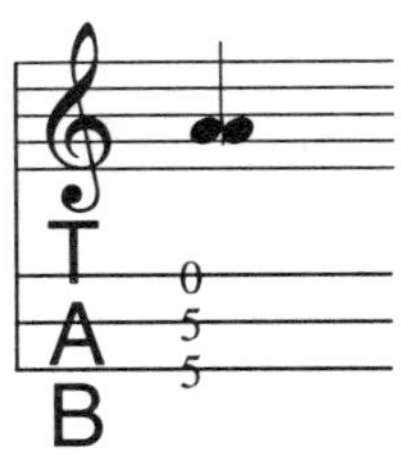

# Holding the Balalaika

The balalaika is played sitting down with the instrument held between the legs [as shown] and the right elbow pressing lightly against the upper corner, thus holding the instrument against the player's body.

The player sits on the edge of the chair. In accordance with tradition the left foot is moved slightly forward.

Ideally, it should be possible to support the instrument in this position without using the left hand; the less the left hand has to support the neck, the greater its freedom in playing.

# The Balalaika Fingerboard

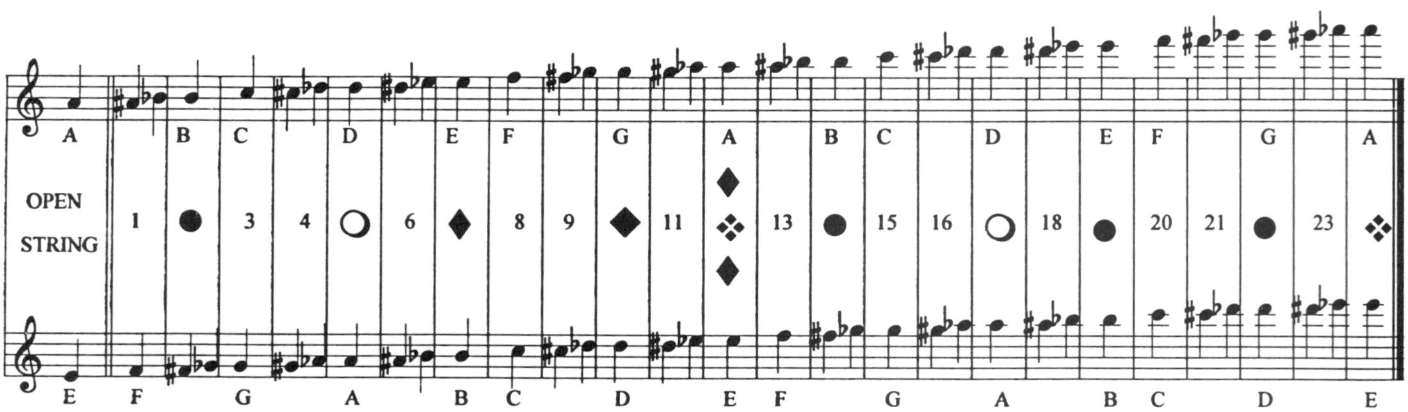

# THE LEFT HAND

The left hand grips the neck of the balalaika between the base of the index finger and the joint between the first and second sections of the thumb, leaving a small space between the hand and the balalaika's neck. The strings are pressed down just behind the frets so that, when plucked, no buzzing is heard. Pressing too lightly or on top of a fret will produce a dull note or buzz.

*The illustration shows the correct method of pressing the string.*

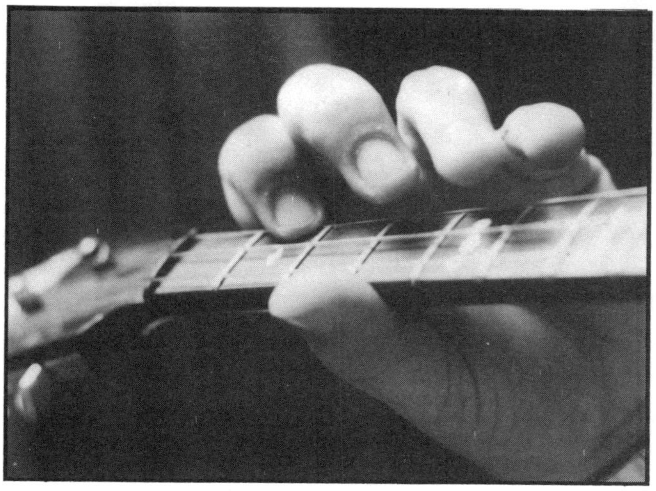

Whenever possible the fingertips should press the strings down from above at an angle perpendicular to the fingerboard. Normally the palm of the left hand should not be flattened against the neck. (An exception to this is when pressing down both the 2nd and 3rd string with the thumb, when the wrist tends to be raised slightly, flattening the hand against the neck.)

When the thumb is not being used to press down a string it should be placed roughly opposite the index/middle finger.

The left elbow is held in against the body. Try not to let it jump sideways during playing.

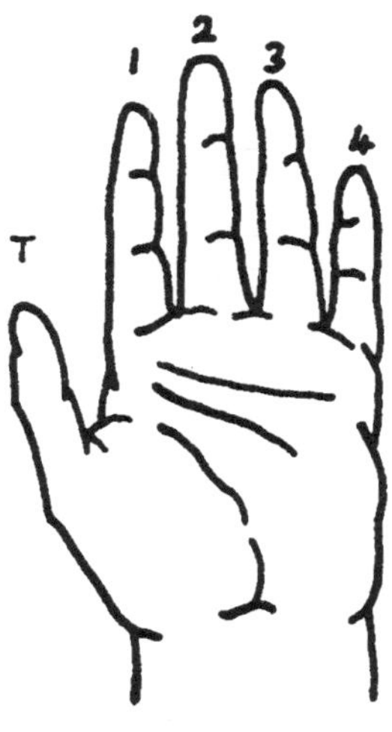


The fingers of the left hand are numbered as shown. In written music, the fingering to be used is marked above the note except where it is considered obvious or when a foregoing pattern is being repeated. In the latter case the word *SIMILE* is sometimes added.

# Strumming with the Thumb

Move the whole forearm together with the hand, brushing the thumb across all three strings and making them sound with equal loudness. This should be a downward sweeping movement – with the fingers extended – brushing along the rim of the scratchplate.

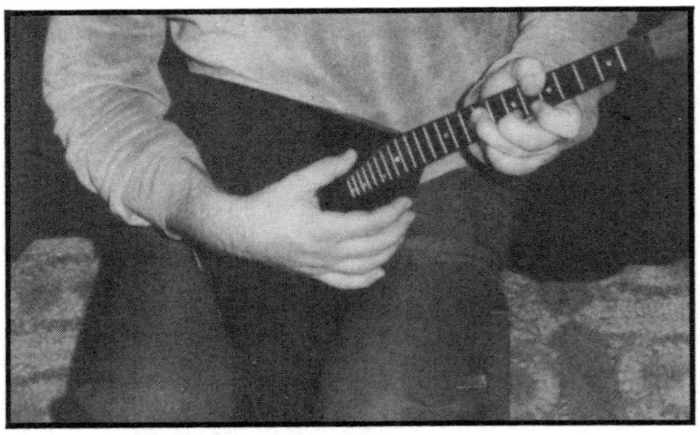

*The R.H. thumb strums across all strings with remaining fingers extended...*

***Play the following examples, practicing both loud and soft playing.***

Exercise 1

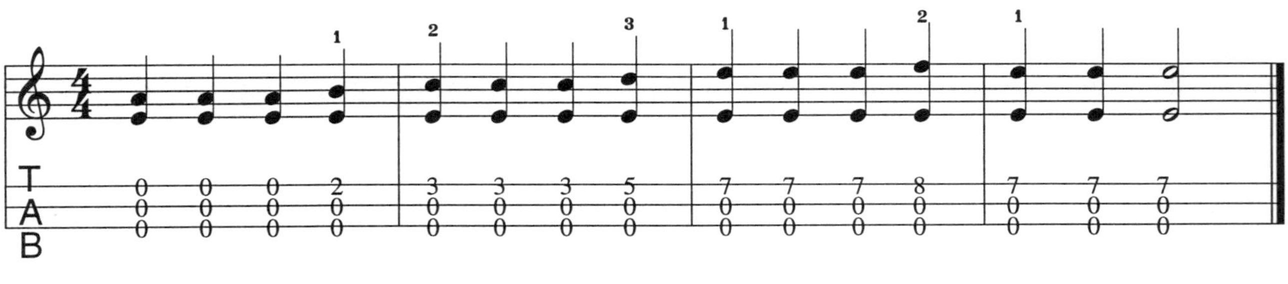

Exercise 2

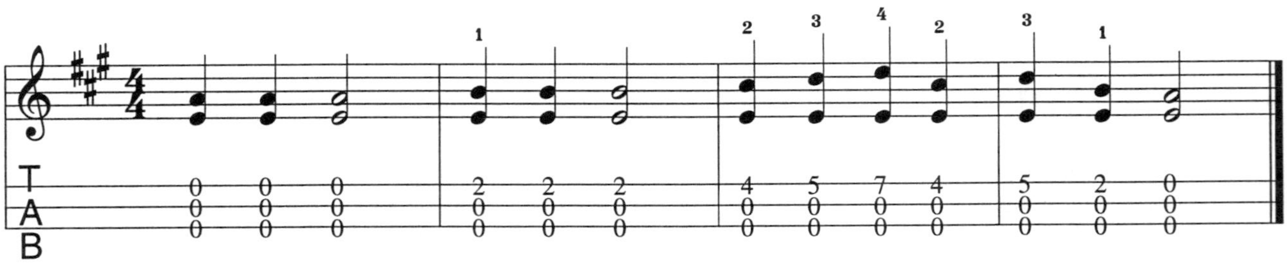

***Note: See page 84 for explanation of tablature***

Strumming all three strings quickly, one after another, is called arpeggiato (harp-like) and in written music is marked with a wavy vertical line before the notes viz:

Exercise 3

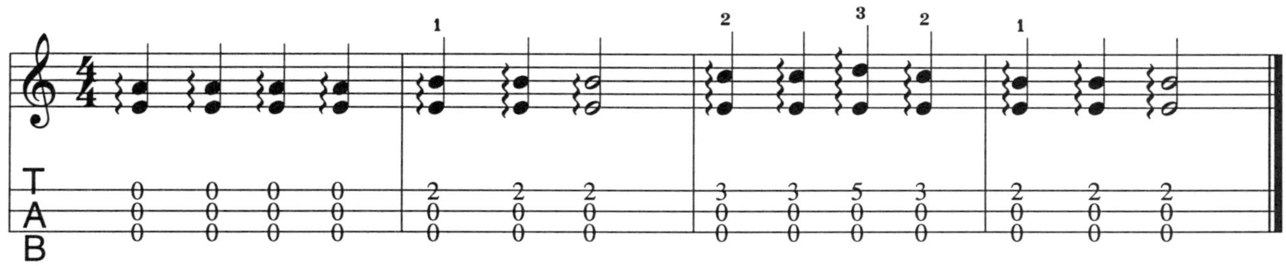


Exercise 4

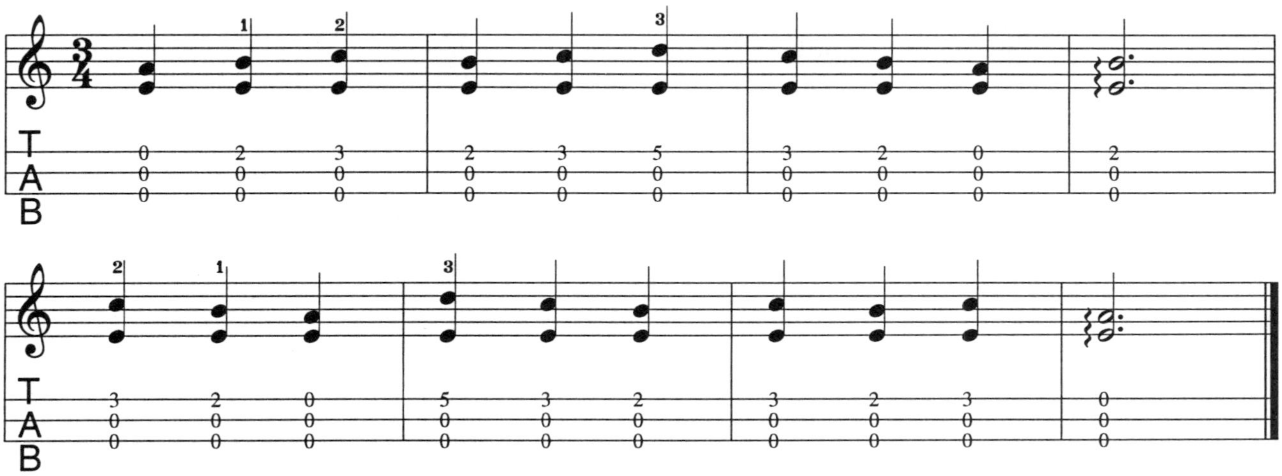


Exercise 5

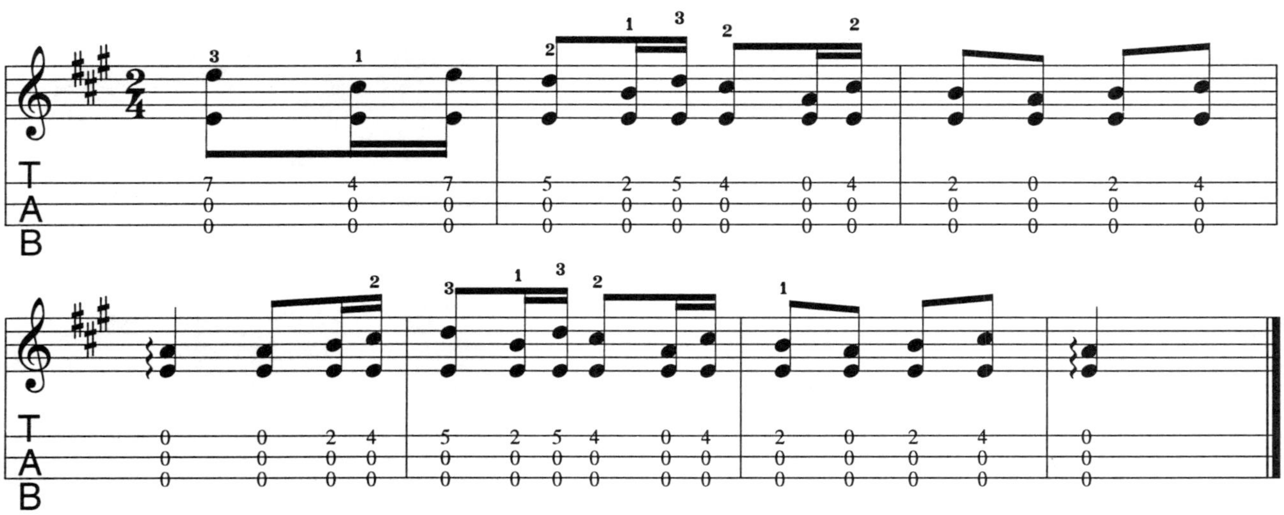

# LEFT HAND: USING THE THUMB

*In stark contrast to accepted Western stringed-instrument playing technique whereby use of the thumb is usually taboo, Russians make great use of their thumbs. (This applies to their native 7-string guitar as well.)*

The thumb is used constantly in balalaika playing. Sometimes it will press down only the third string, leaving the second string open. A lot of the time it will be covering both the second and third strings and will, moreover, jump from one fret to another independently of what the other fingers are doing on the top string. This will require some getting used to.

It is important that the thumb be trained to firmly press both strings down behind the fret correctly, producing not only a note of the correct pitch but also a clear tone, free of buzzing. Check this by plucking each string individually before striking all strings together.

The left wrist can be raised upwards and the hand flattened slightly to allow sufficient pressure to be applied to the two E strings. However, the hand should not be twisted round too far: this will tend to flatten the remaining fingers, thereby adversely affecting the playing on the top string.

Also avoid inadvertently raising the pitch of one or other of these notes by pushing either of these strings sideways with the thumb.

*Illustration shows the thumb pressing two strings at a time.*

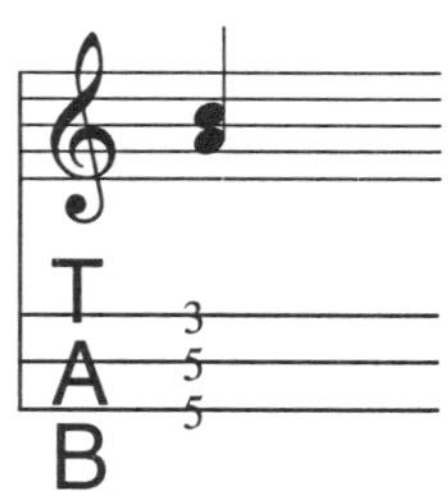


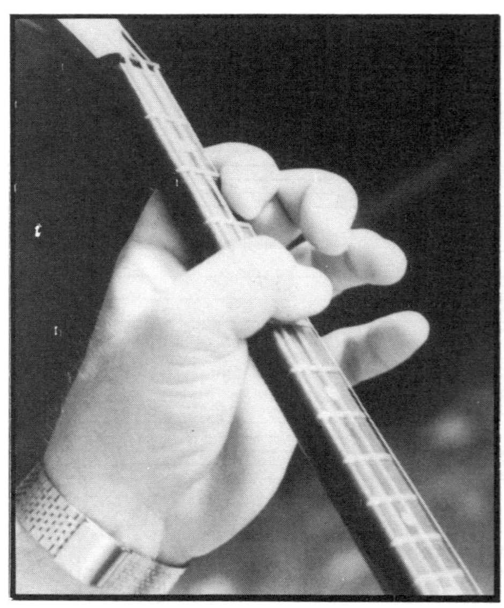

*The thumb presses both the second and third strings throughout most of "Daydreams" below and isn't marked. Note also that as the fingering for the first few bars of "Daydreams" is the same, it isn't marked for each successive note. This saves "cluttering" the music with unnecessary symbols.*

Exercise 6

"Daydreams" ("Ґрезы") – by V.V. Andreyev (excerpt)

Exercise 7

"Wlazl Kotek" (Cat on the Fence) – *Polish Nursery Rhyme*

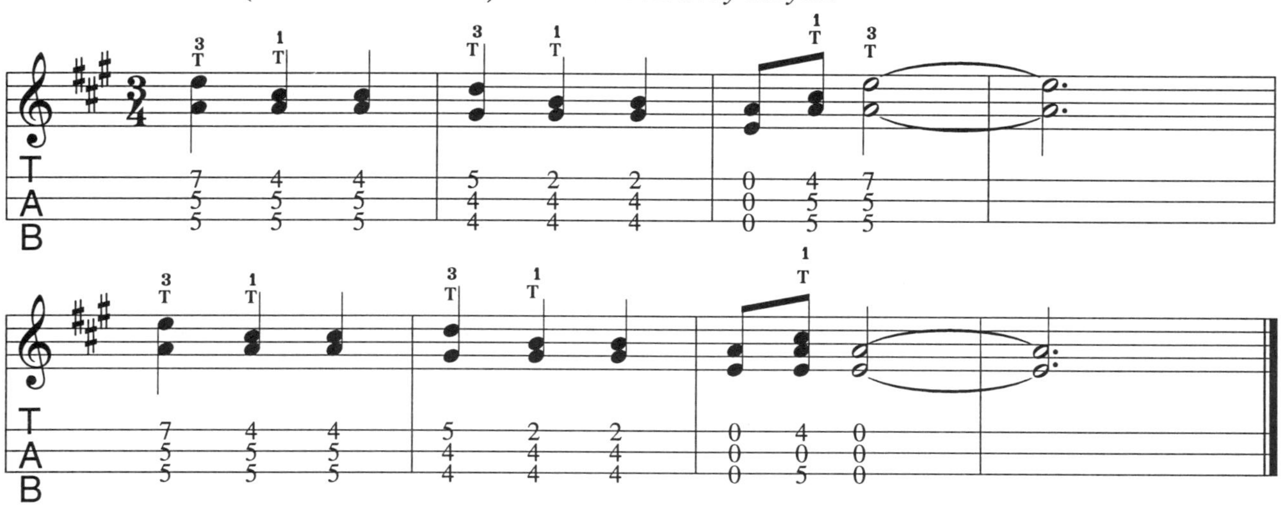

The marking for the thumb ("T" in this tutor, "б" in Russian music) is often omitted from fingering when its use is considered obvious.

# Right Hand: Plucking With the Thumb

With the hand held still, the extended fingers hold the lower edge of the scratchplate while the thumb moves across to pluck individual strings. Alternately, the whole hand may move slightly with the thumb movement to produce a slightly different sound.

On one string this style is used for the slow passages only (at high speed the hand quickly tires).

*With this technique as with all others in this book, make up exercises similar to those provided and practice them thoroughly, making sure that each note sounds clearly.*

Exercise 8

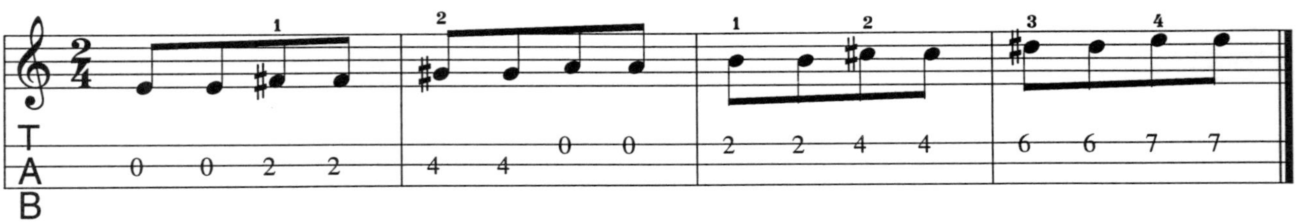


Exercise 9

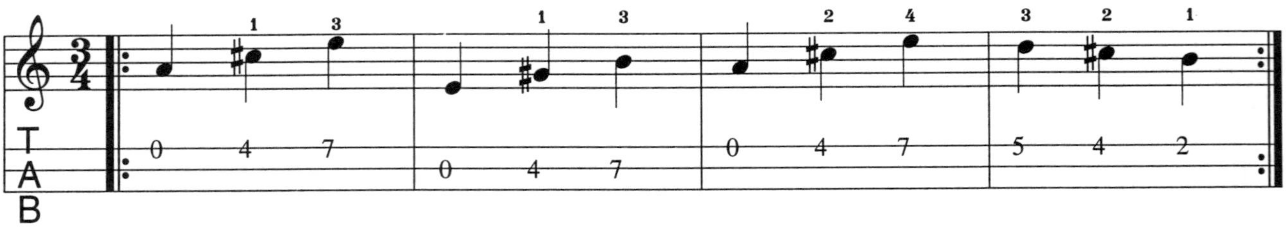


***Play the following piece, strumming section 2 with the thumb and (for now) ignoring the markings above the notes.***

Exercise 10

"In the Garden, in the Orchard" – ("Vo sadu li, v ogorode") *Russian Folk Song*

# Strumming With the Index Finger

This consists of striking all three strings simultaneously with the extended index finger in a combination of down- and up-strokes. Along with *tremolo* this is the most important balalaika stroke and once mastered will form the basis for learning most other techniques employed in playing the balalaika.

The index finger is extended, slightly bent and the remaining fingers are curled up with the thumb lightly resting on the middle or index finger.

The thumb must not stick out. With the wrist bent and above all **completely relaxed**, the forearm is raised and then with a small sharp movement downward flings the index finger down across the strings. The hand acts like a deadweight due to the loose wrist.[1]

The strings are strummed at about the 19th fret and it is the fleshy fingertip which touches the string, not the nail. The hand should be held in such a way that the nail is not pointing downwards, but faces towards the top of the neck, causing the fingertip to strike sideways across the strings.

Upward movement of the forearm brings the finger back up across the strings to the starting position, ready for the next down-stroke.

## When practicing, aim to achieve:

- even-sounding down-strokes
- down- and up-strokes identical in tone and volume
- ability to play even-sounding combinations of the above
- ability to accentuate any stroke in the pattern at will without destroying the evenness of the remaining strokes

[1] Imagine flicking a drop of water from the tip of the index finger.

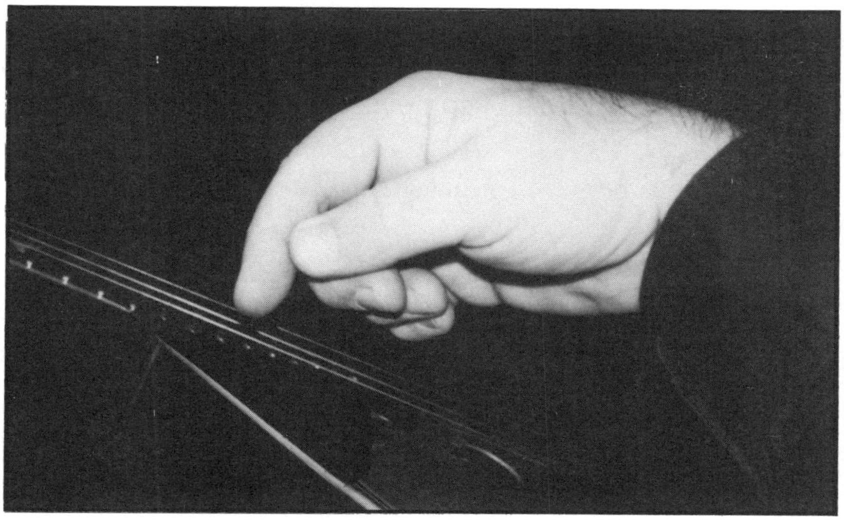

*How the index finger is held*

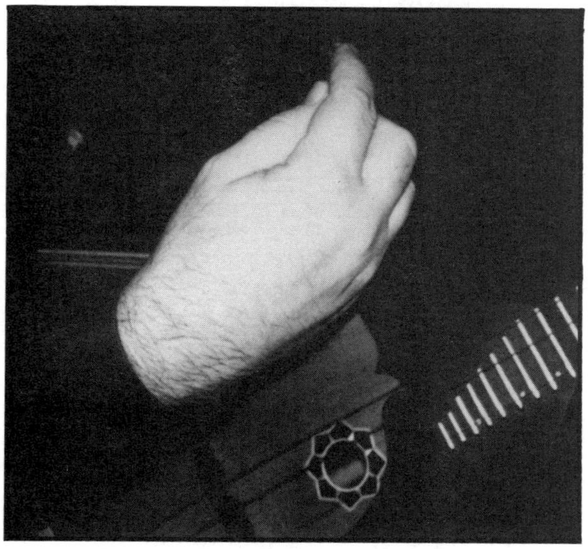

*The starting position*

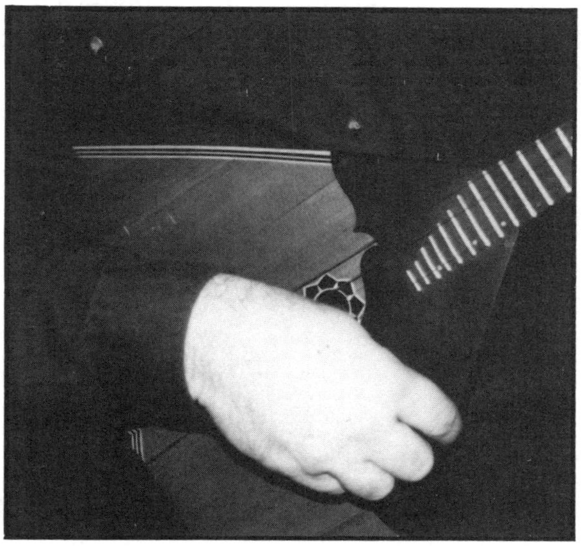

*The finishing position*

*(In reality the wrist muscles stiffen ever so slightly to hold the index finger at the correct angle during the up-stroke. However, the player should make a conscious effort to maintain the overall relaxed state of the wrist throughout.)*

In the early stages of learning rhythmic strumming and in particular tremolo (see next section), the wrist will constantly display a tendency to stiffen up. Speeding up a series of down/up strokes will even cause the wrist to completely "seize-up" and the hand and forearm to move together in one line before stopping altogether. This is only because the muscles have not yet learned to coordinate themselves properly. That takes time and, above all, patient and regular practice.

When practicing down- and up-strokes, one should play slowly at first, then gradually faster, focusing attention on total relaxation of the wrist. As soon as it begins to stiffen, stop and shake it to make sure it is completely loose; then start again.

At the same time be sure that the up-strokes sound equal in volume and tone to the down-strokes.

Strummed passages for the balalaika almost invariably consist of a varying combination of down- and up-strokes. Sometimes down- or up-strokes are accentuated (marked with > above the note). The often highly intricate patterns of alternating down- and up-strokes with certain notes being accentuated give the particular dynamic, bubbly effect so characteristic of the balalaika.

The above effect can only be achieved if one has first mastered a perfectly even down- and up-stroke and is able to accentuate whichever stroke is desired without upsetting the timing. A mistake common among careless beginners at the balalaika is running a whole series of notes together into an almost continuous alternation of down- and up-strokes rather than breaking the passage up into a pattern of down followed by down/up-strokes. The following examples will illustrate this point more clearly.

Exercise 11

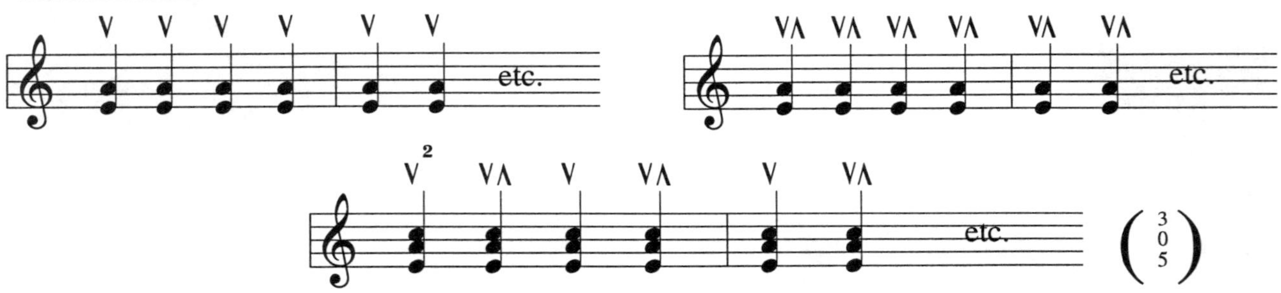


With strumming, the number of strokes per note depends on the character and speed of the piece and is usually indicated as shown here. When it isn't, the player must decide. The first note of each bar is usually slightly accentuated with a DOWN-stroke, even when this is not indicated. *(See Daily Exercises on p. 76 )*

Exercise 12

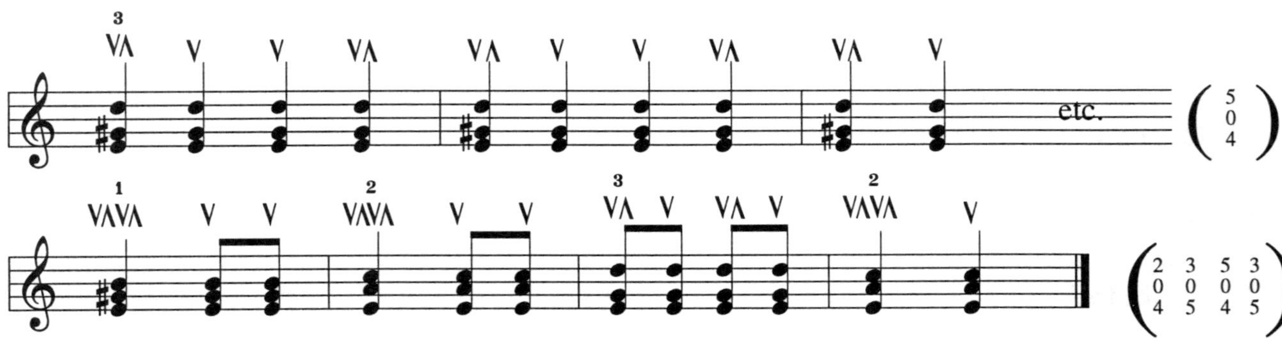


***Practice "In The Garden..." as before but use rhythmic strumming in Section 2.***

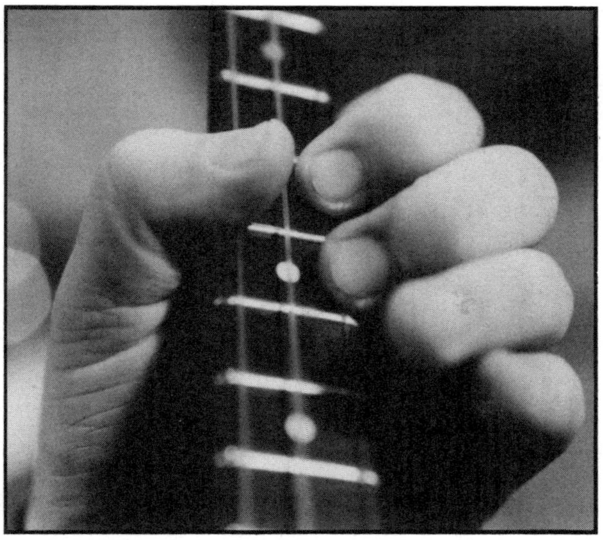

A-major 

$E_7$ 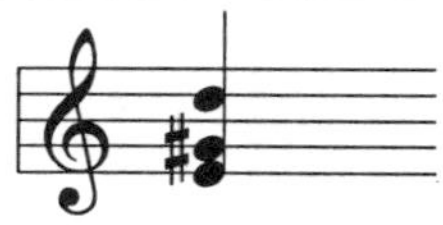

Exercise 13

Russian Polka

*(Simile: same strokes as in preceding passage)*

# Annotation of Strokes

There are two different systems most commonly used for indicating the down- and up-strokes. One system is the same as that used for violin bowing, namely ⊓ for down stroke and V for up. The other, which makes more immediate sense to the balalaika player is, V for down and Λ for up.[1] In this tutor the self-explanatory arrow markings are used.

The Pedlar's Box (Korobushka) - *Russian Folk Song*

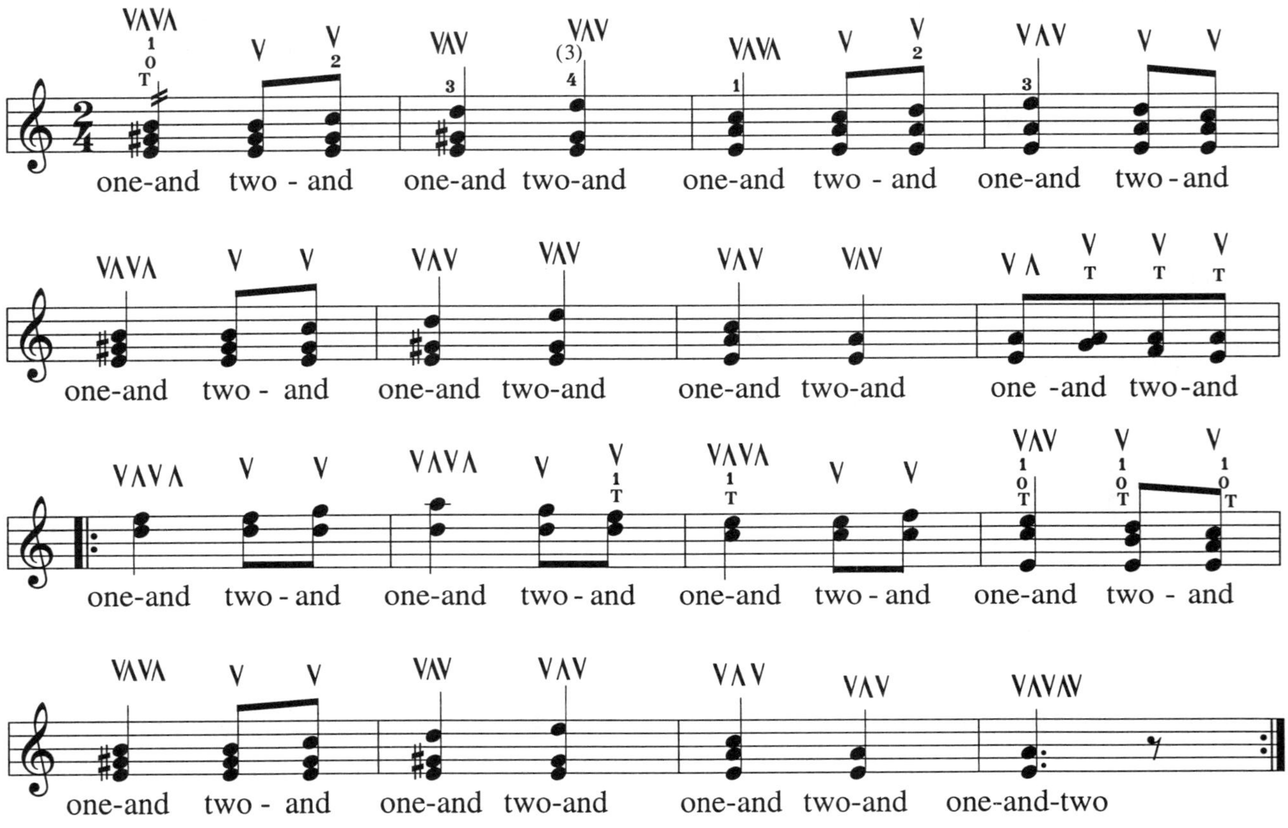


---

[1] One may occasionally come across balalaika music using a third system where the direction of strokes is marked ´ for down and ` for up. The brainchild of Professors Gelis and Ye. Blinov, formerly of the Kiev Conservatoire, this system seems confined to Sverdlovsk and the Ukraine, where it is widely used. Other signs used by this system are: ∠ - *stroke with the thumb;* • – *pizz. with middle finger.*

It is hard to see the logic in this system and such music is often preceded by an explanatory note. Given the inevitable confusion the use of the first two equally-popular systems occasionally creates, the very existence of a third system seems ludicrous.

**Strumming**: In addition to down/up markings above the note, *strumming* may also be indicated with one or two short slanted lines through the note stem.[1]

> ***One short line*** indicates the note is to be played as a series of eighth notes (quavers), the single line representing the single tail (flag) of an eighth note.
>
> ***Two short lines*** indicate the note is to be played as a series of sixteenth notes (semi-quavers), the two lines representing the double flag of a sixteenth note.

A single short line through an eighth note stem indicates that two sixteenth notes are to be played. (i.e.: the eighth note flag plus the line = the double flag of a sixteenth note).

**Tremolo** is indicated by the word *trem.* (*трем.*) at the beginning of a tremoloed section or – especially in mixed-stroke passages – by **three** short, slanted lines through the note stem.[2] Occasionally tremolo is indicated by a curved legato mark – *a ligature* – above a series of notes.

"Concert Variations" - P. Kulikov

---

[1] Surprisingly, this important feature is almost never explained in balalaika tutors, Russian (Soviet) or otherwise.

[2] As compared with the *four* short lines for tremolo usual in standard Western notation.
*Two* short slanted lines instead of three are used with tremoloed eighth notes (quavers), the note's own *flag* or *tail* being the equivalent of the third short line. (e.g.: "Concert Variations" - P. Kulikov, bars 95-96.)
*Three* short slanted lines have on rare occasions been used to indicate strumming. See: "Pivna Yagoda" – B. Troyanovsky, bar 61 – a quarter note (crotchet) divided into eight 32nd notes (demi-semi quavers), (4 down, 4 up).

# Tremolo

Tremolo consists of an uninterrupted series of fast alternating down- and up-strokes played across all strings with the tip of the index finger, giving the impression of continuous sound.

It is this uniquely soft, haunting sound produced by the fingertip (rather than with a plectrum) with which the balalaika is so romantically associated.

As with strumming, it is essential that the upward and downward strokes be identical in both volume and tone and initially a great deal of attention must be paid to this point.

Learning the tremolo further highlights even more the need for a completely loose wrist. The beginner, not to be discouraged, should realize that it will probably take up to a year to achieve a smooth tremolo, unbroken by unintentional "misses." The player should aim for a perfect tremolo that can be varied in volume from very soft to very loud at will.

*In tremolo the hand is usually held much like for strumming, except that the Thumb may release the index finger - as shown here.*

Exercise 14

"Steppes All Around" - *Russian Folk Song*

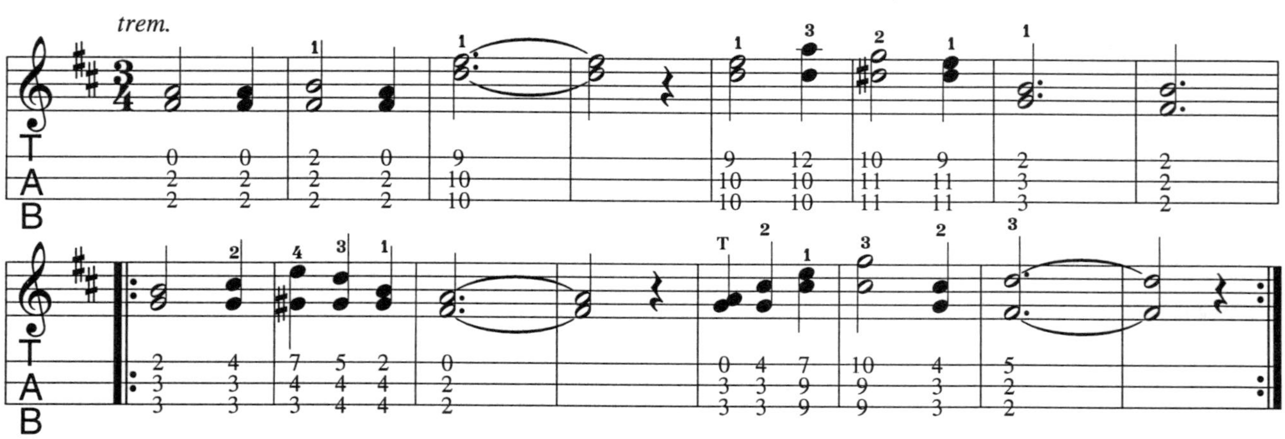

**Tremolo, unlike Strumming, does not entail a strictly fixed number of strokes.**[1]
This will be dictated by the speed of the piece and the player's judgement and skill. Once tremolo becomes second nature, the adept player will neither have to think about nor count the strokes; their frequency will be adjusted automatically.
The usual number of strokes per note is shown in the chart and example below.

| The number of whole strokes per value of note is generally as follows: | | | | |
|---|---|---|---|---|
| Whole note | (Semi-breve) | = 24 down | and | 24 up-strokes |
| Half note | (Minim) | = 12 down | and | 12 up-strokes |
| Quarter note | (Crotchet) | = 6 down | and | 6 up-strokes |
| Eighth note | (Quaver) | = 3 down | and | 3 up-strokes |
| Sixteenth note | (Semi-quaver) | = 2 down | and | 1 up-stroke[2] |
| Any dotted notes have an additional 50 percent value (e.g.: a dotted quarter note = 9 down- and 9 up-strokes) | | | | |

*Tremolo - realistic frequency of down/up strokes:*

should be played:

Exercise 15

"Evening Bell" - *Russian Folk Song*

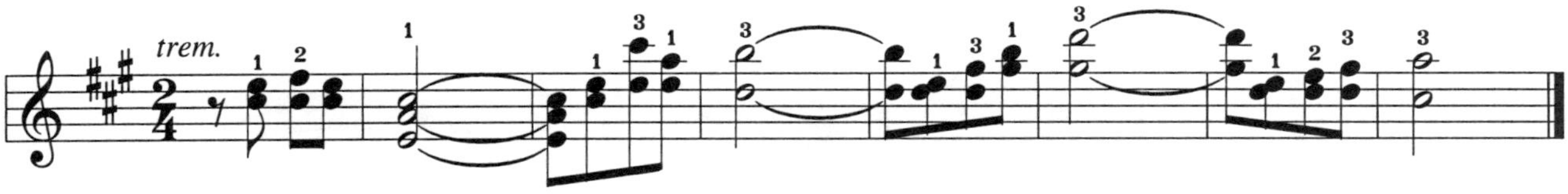


[1] For example, a tremoloed quarter note may consist of anything between 4 - 8 sets of down/up strokes.

[2] Or 1 down- and 2 up -strokes.

Tam na Bloniu - *Polish Folk Song*

"Oh you, lassie" (Oi ty, divchyno) - *Ukranian Folk Song*

***Play Andreyev's "Daydreams" through again using first rhythmic strumming, then tremolo. (see p. 7)***

Russian Sailor's Dance - (Yablochko)

"Goin' Home"

"The Slender Rowan Tree" (Tonkaya Ryabina) - *Russian folk song*

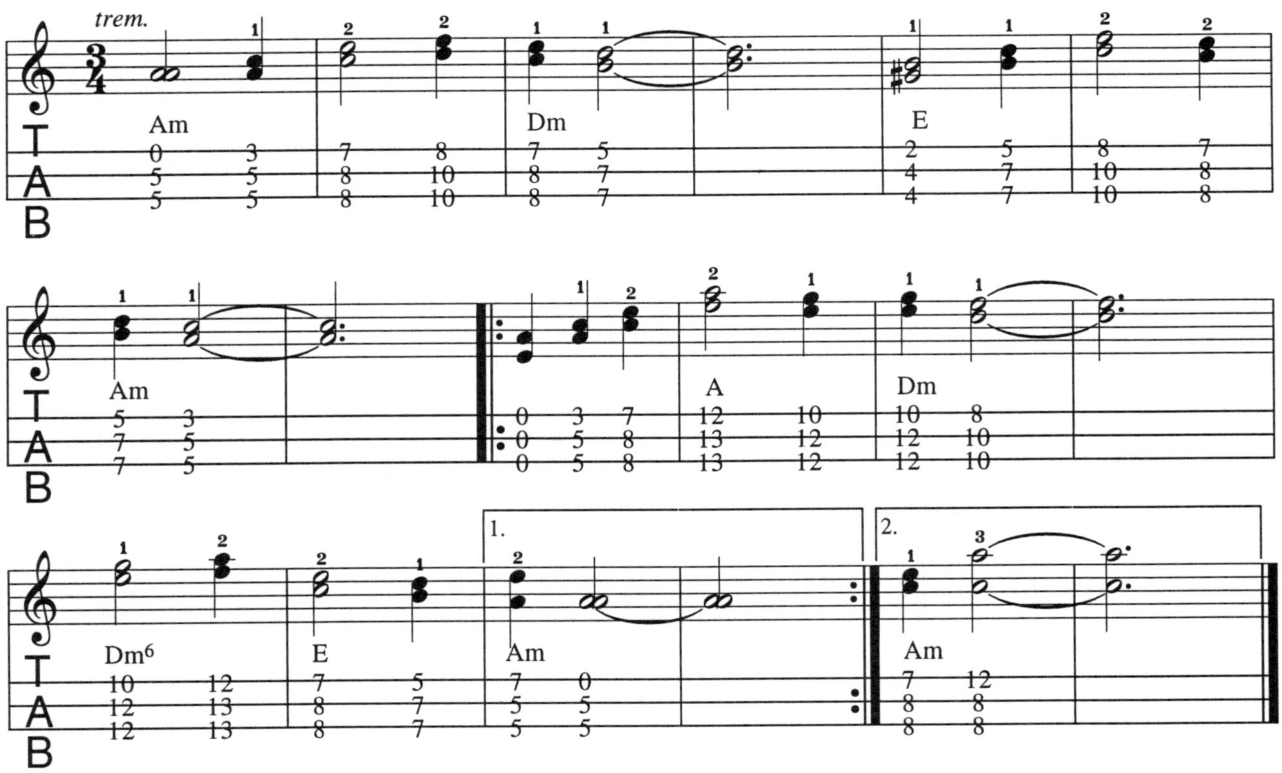


"Wheelbarrows in the Rain" (Tachki na dozhde) - Bibs Ekkel

# Tremolo on 2nd and 3rd Strings Only

By altering the angle and shortening the stroke of the right-hand index finger, it is possible to tremolo on just the 2nd and 3rd strings together. To assist in this slightly awkward operation the little finger of the left hand is extended to lightly touch the top (A) string, thus effectively deadening it against being sounded by any stray strokes.

Exercise 16

The thumb plays the 3rd string and often isn't marked in the music.

Some of the following melodies have been provided with guitar accompaniment chords.

Exercise 17

"I Loved You" (Ya vas lubil) - Count Sheremyetev

"Varyag" - *Russian folk song*

"I was in the Garden" (Ya v sadochke byla) - *Russian folk song*

*(See also Tremolo on one string* p. 35 )

# Double Pizzicato

Although the thumb alone may be adequate for plucking (pizzicato) downward on one string at slow speeds, for faster passages down/up strokes are required. The down-stroke is played by the thumb and the up-stroke by the index finger. This technique is known among balalaika players as double pizzicato.

Both finger and thumb are held stiffly and must not move in relation to one another. Movement comes from the relaxed wrist in addition to slight movement from the forearm.

*(At first the finger and thumb will have a tendency to move to pluck the string. Avoid letting this become a habit - as both speed and volume will eventually suffer.)*

The remaining fingers may be bunched up or extended to brush the scratchplate and provide a level for the two playing fingers. Whichever method you choose is a question of individual preference. There are also slight variations between players in the way the thumb and index finger are held. Some actually cross the thumb and index finger, but most hold them apart (see next illustration). The latter is recommended.

The distance with which the thumb and index finger are held apart may vary from player to player and may also vary depending on the character and speed of the passage being played.

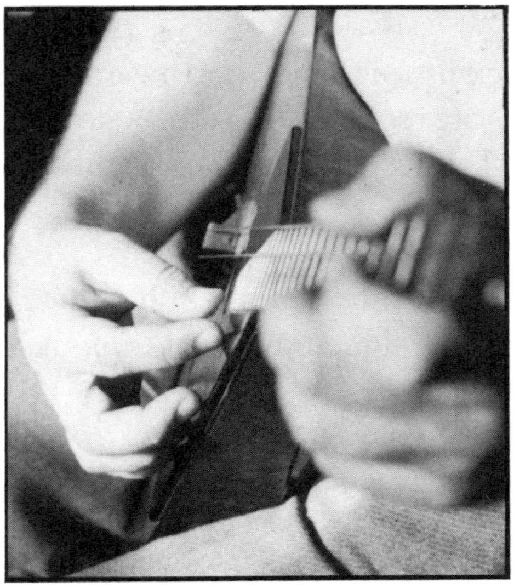

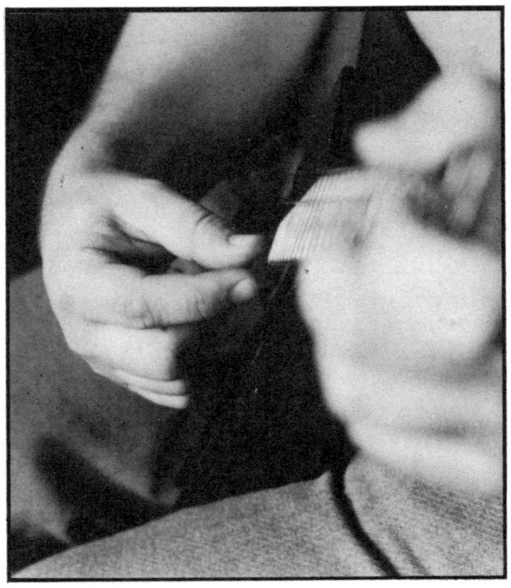

*The remaining fingers may be extended . . . . . . . . . . . . . . . . . or tucked away.*

Exercise 18

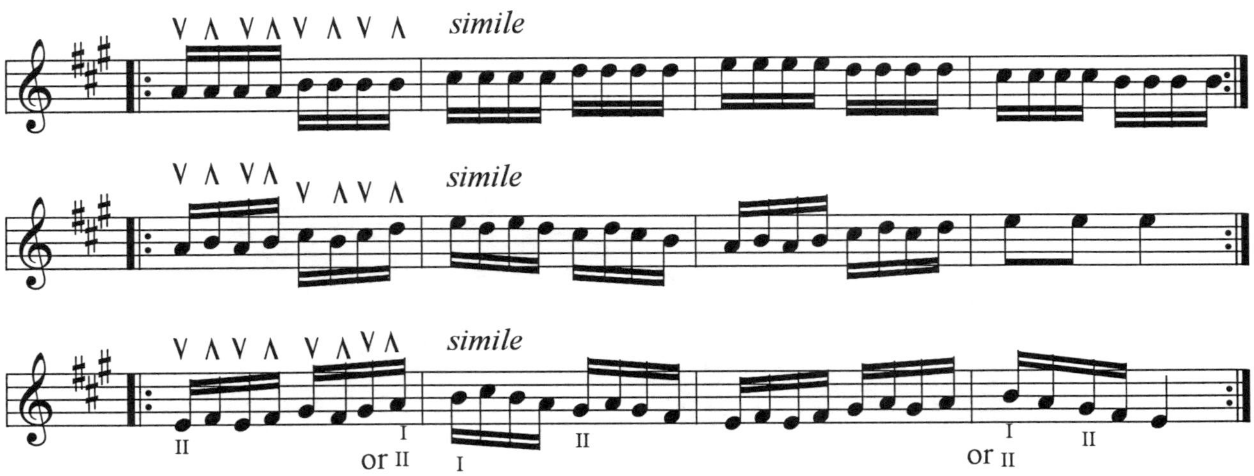


A Roman numeral below the note is often used to indicate the string being played. (In some older balalaika music "sul A" or "E" is used instead.)

Exercise 19

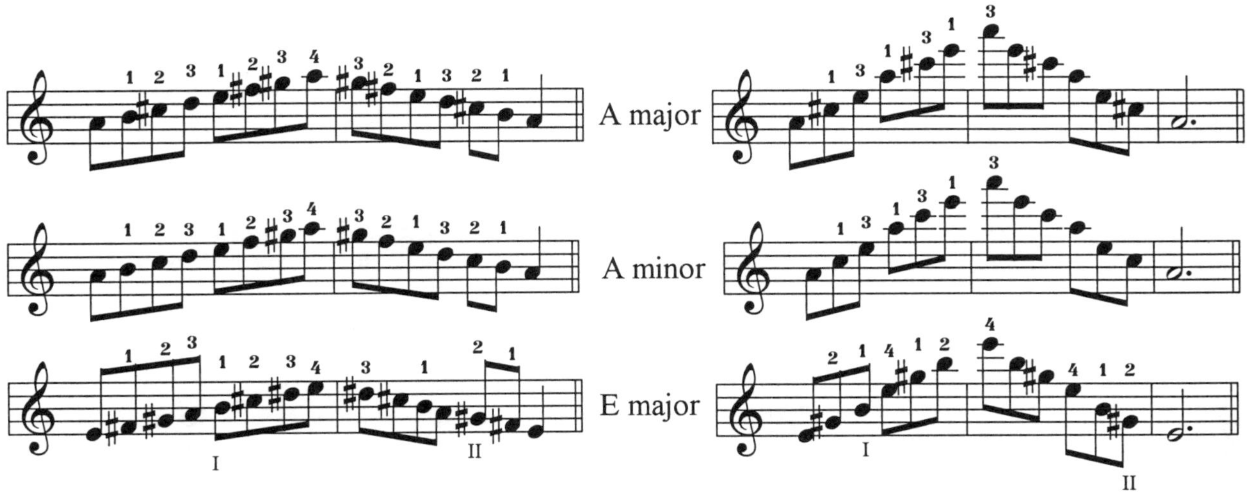


Double pizzicato may be used to intermittently pluck one of the other strings in alternation with the top string.

Exercise 20

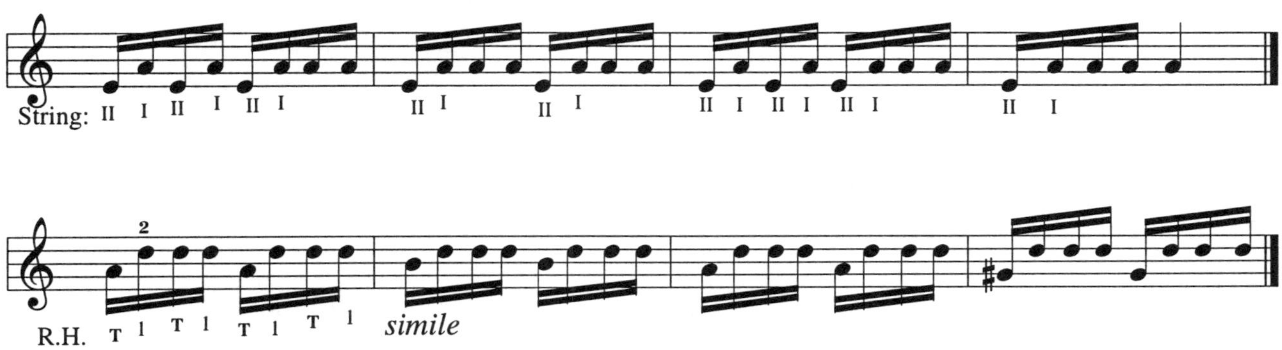


The 2nd or 3rd string may be made to ring longer, thus:

Exercise 21

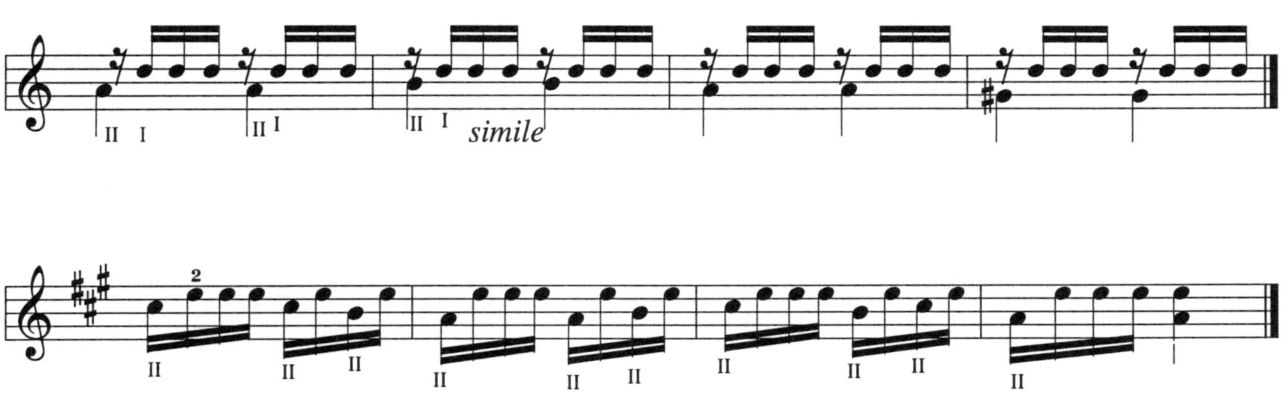


*(Note that when playing the III instead of II string, pressing down with the left-hand thumb becomes easier as it no longer has to cover two strings; but at the same time the right hand has to work harder moving further to reach over the 2nd string without touching it. In the above examples, accuracy may be helped by the right hand moving forward – in the direction of the neck – for the thumb to play the 2nd string. When plucking the 3rd string, this forward movement would be still more pronounced to help the thumb avoid touching the middle string.)*

***Practice the preceding examples again using the 3rd instead of the 2nd string.***

Exercise 22

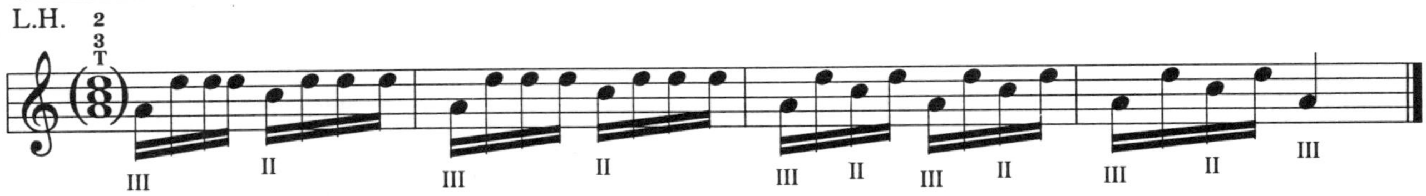


Exercise 23

In the above two examples an A-minor chord is held down (shown in brackets).
The R.H. thumb alternates between the three strings.

When the player eventually attains a high speed of double pizzicato, the technique may be used to tremolo on one string.

Exercise 24

*(Having the middle string moved over slightly towards the 3rd string, as recommended earlier, facilitates single-string pizzicato and tremolo on the 1st and 2nd strings.)*

The Willow Tree - (Ivushka) *Russian Folk Song*

In the third bar from the end in the above piece a barre has to be used, whereby the index finger flattens out to press the first as well as the second string.

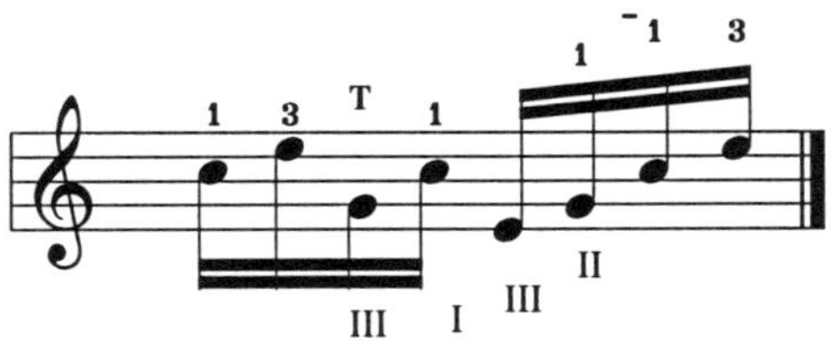

Barres are rarely used on the balalaika, and then only when no effective alternative exists.

With the middle string moved over off-centre towards the third string (as recommended and described in detail in the foreword), *double pizzicato* on the middle string should present no particular problem – with the following exception.

## Difficulties with the up-stroke on the middle string:

In fast pizzicato passages, it can be a little awkward to follow a down-stroke (with the thumb) on the top string with an up-stroke (with the index finger) on the middle string. In descending passages involving a switch from the first to the second string it is usually preferable that the first note on the middle string be with a down-stroke. This is a principle to be kept in mind when working out fingering. Compare the two following examples:

Exercise 25

Compare:

with:

An up-stroke with the index finger on the middle string becomes still more awkward in passages where the thumb is used to alternately pluck the 1st and 3rd strings. In having to reach over the middle string without touching it the thumb *has* to move, and the rules governing the immobility of the thumb and index finger relative to each other are broken. Both fingers end up having to move, and as a consequence speed is lost.

Exercise 26

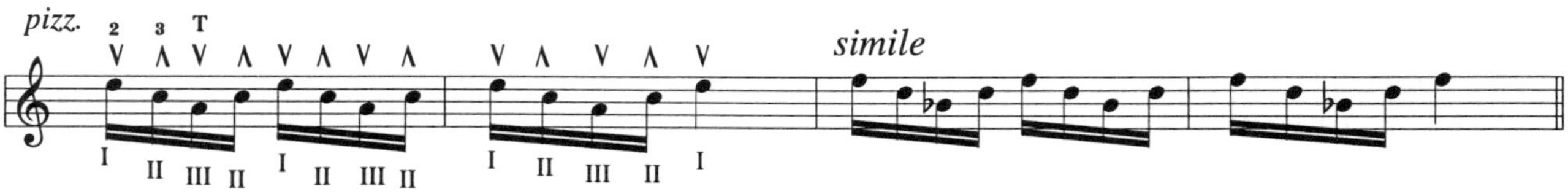


The above passage would more normally be played:

*(See also: "Extra Difficult Strokes" on p. 71)*

# Single Pizzicato

Another way of playing pizzicato on one string is with the index finger only, the tip of which is either supported by the thumb (see illustration) or gripped between thumb and middle finger like a plectrum.

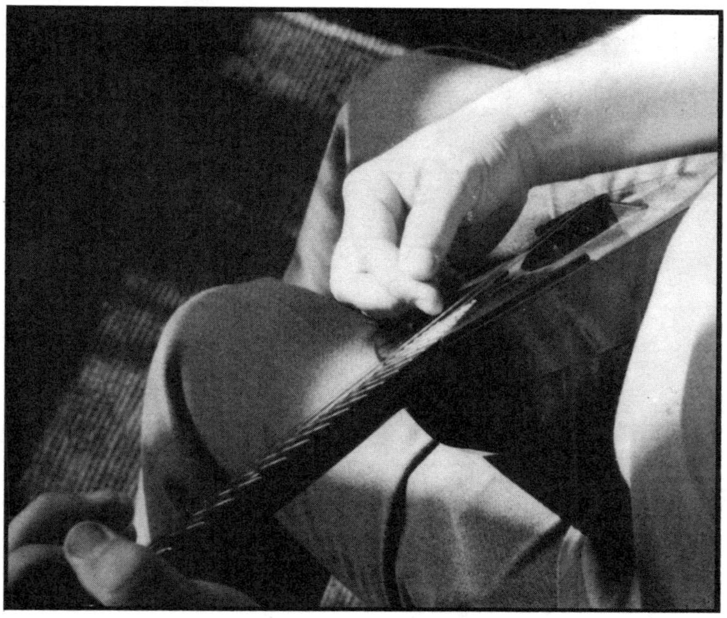

*The thumb supports the index finger.*

The downward stroke is angled towards the scratchplate which the index finger touches at the end of the stroke; the upward stroke is angled so as to miss the second string. The wrist is bent and loose and the remaining fingers may be loosely curled up, the little finger acting as a leveller for the playing finger by brushing the scratchplate during playing, or, as with double pizzicato, the remaining fingers may be straightened to brush the scratchplate.

This technique is used particularly for very fast scalelike pizzicato passages (e.g.: Rimsky-Korsakov's "Flight of the Bumble-Bee"). However, many players develop a personal preference for either single or double pizzicato, resorting to the other technique only when obliged to do so by the nature of the particular passage.

Exercise 27

***Play through the following passages making sure the strokes all sound even. Practice to get the tone and volume of the down- and up-strokes to sound the same.***

Exercise 28

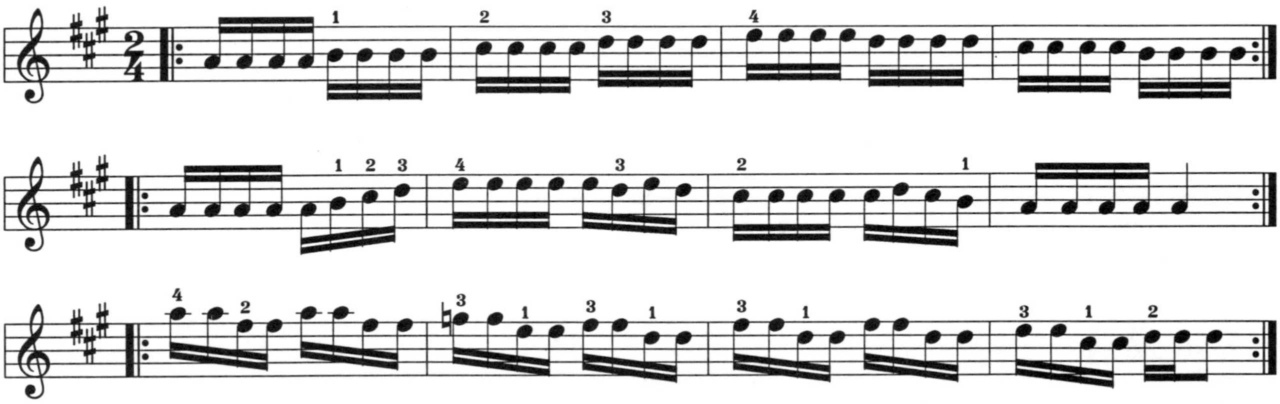

from "Valenki" - A. Shirokov

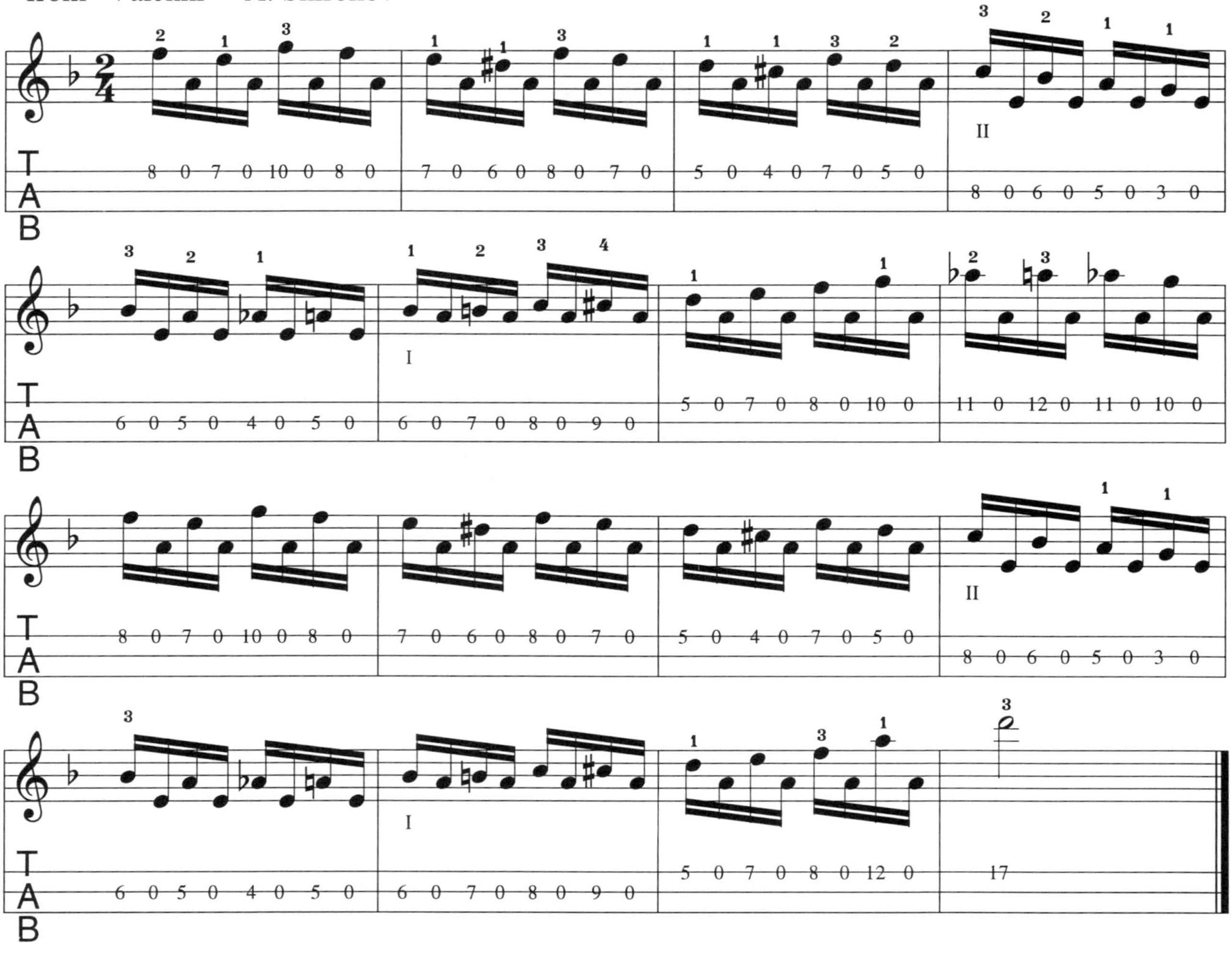

# Pizzicato & the Left Hand

The melody line is usually played on the top (steel) string on the balalaika. Fast variations are often executed exclusively on the top string as an occasional note struck on a nylon string can sound out of place, due to the different tone of the nylon strings. Because of this the left hand does a lot of jumping from one position to another on the neck – far more than would be the case when executing the same passage on, say, a violin or mandolin, where the other strings would be used. (Examples of this and the fingering involved can be found in the section dealing with double pizzicato.)

For the study of most other stringed instruments a system of numbered positions is used for the left hand. According to this system, No. 1 position would be when the index finger is on the second fret, No. 2 position on the third fret, No. 3 on the fifth fret, etc., with a relative number of half-positions: the difference between positions and half-positions depending on the key of the piece being played. As the main advantage of "positional playing" is gained when playing single note passages involving more than one string, the system has little practical application to the balalaika.

On the balalaika fast pizzicato passages are usually played entirely on the top string, travelling onto the 2nd string only when ultimately necessary.

The "position" of the hand is clear from the fingering indicated - following the general rule that the thumb, when not actually pressing a string, is placed roughly opposite the index/ middle finger.

***Practice the following examples slowly at first. Pay close attention to the accurate flow of notes between the two different left-hand positions involved. The transition from one position to another should be quick, accurate, and inaudible, with the whole hand jumping to exactly the right new position for playing the next few notes and landing with the thumb positioned correctly opposite the index/ middle finger.***

*(Think of the hand as a typewriter carriage.)*

Exercise 29

Exercise 30

Exercise 31

## Fingering

The fingering in fast pizzicato passages is critical. Very often the fingering will have to be carefully worked out to allow for maximum ease and comfort in playing and to avoid smudged notes or the fingers tripping over each other. Consider the following examples:

Exercise 32

WORSE

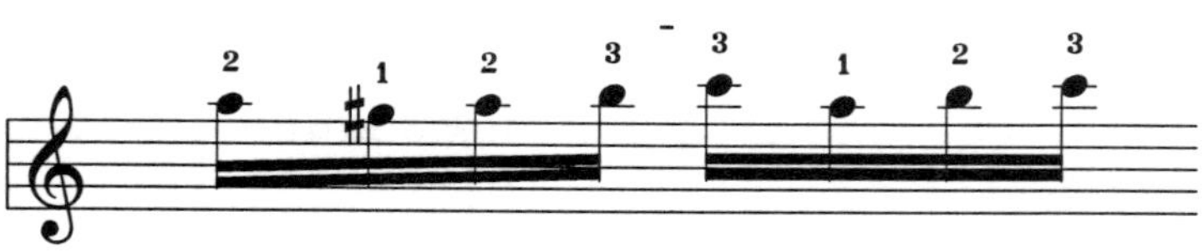

BETTER

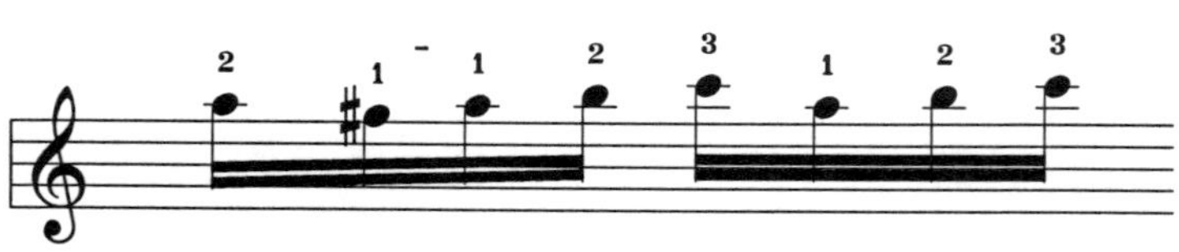

Because the 1st finger is stronger than the 3rd it is usually the better finger to use to slide to a new position, affording a cleaner, more accurate transition at speed.

"Flight of the Bumble Bee" (excerpt) - Rimsky-Korsakov

*(As with all strokes involving a loose wrist, the slower the speed, the wider the swing; the faster the speed, the smaller the swing.)*

Exercise 33

"Morning Etude" - Bibs Ekkel

Sometimes when playing single pizzicato, it may become necessary to switch to double pizzicato for the playing of only a couple of notes (for example while switching from the A to the E string or vice versa). In these cases *pizz.1* or *pizz.2* may be marked in the music to distinguish between the recommended use of single or double pizzicato.

Song of the Plains (Poliushko-Pole) - Knipper

from "Valenki" - A. Shirokov

***Try the above examples again using double instead of single pizzicato.***

# Tremolo on One String

There are two ways a tremolo on one string can be achieved. One way – speeding up double pizzicato to produce a tremolo – can be quite difficult.

The more common way is with just the index finger, which is held just as in single pizzicato (either with the thumb or thumb and middle finger supporting it). Much practice will be needed to achieve not only a smooth tremolo without breaks, but one with down- and up-strokes sounding even in both tone and volume.

Once this stroke has been mastered, the player can go on to learn Tremolo-Vibrato, a unique and effective balalaika sound. *(see p. 40)*

Exercise 34

Exercise 35

Oh you, the Night - (Akh ty, Nochenka) - *Russian Folk Song*

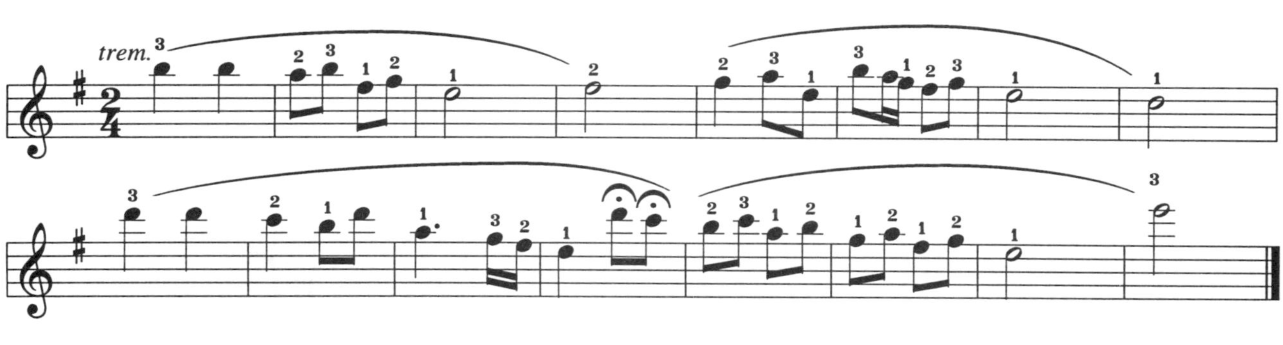


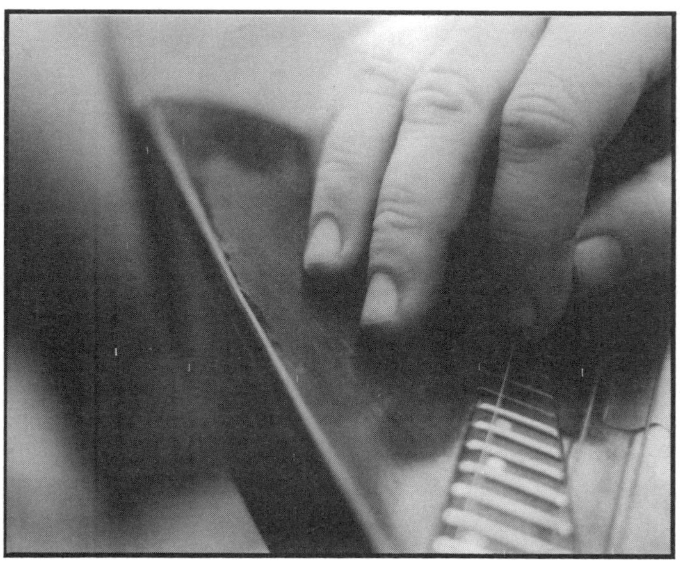

# VIBRATO

Vibrato is an effect produced when the note is "vibrated" up and down (alternately raised and lowered) immediately after being played. On other stringed instruments this is usually done with a shaking movement of the left hand while pressing down the string. On the balalaika, it is achieved by using the heel of the right hand to alternately press down on the bridge (thus lowering the note) and press on the part of the A string between the bridge and end-piece (raising the note).

*For vibrato the string is plucked UPWARDS with the extended index (or middle) finger.*

**There are two basic types of vibrato:** In one, the heel of the right hand is placed so that one part (marked B in the diagram) rests on the 2nd and 3rd strings, on or just below the bridge. The base of the little finger (marked A in the diagram) touches the section of the A-string between the bridge and lower nut.

*As the A-string is plucked, the right hand is waggled from side to side in a pivoting motion, alternately applying pressure to the two points and thus vibrating the note.*

This is called "**true**" vibrato as it "vibrates" about the true note (above and below it).

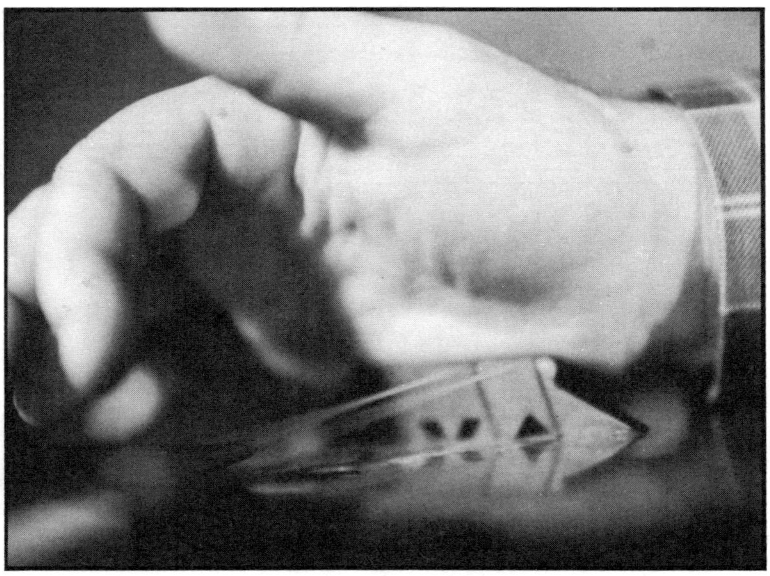

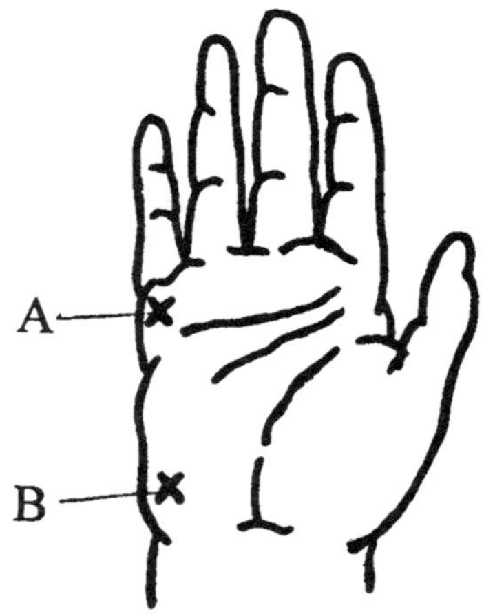


***Photo & Diagram:*** *Points on the palm of the right hand that vibrate the string. In "true" vibrato, point A vibrates the A-string, point B - the E-strings. In "false" vibrato, point B vibrates the A-string.*

A vibrato may also be played with the heel of the right hand pressing only on the A string beyond the bridge without pressing down on the bridge itself. This produces what is known as **"false"** vibrato, so called as the note is raised above the original pitch but not lowered below it, thus giving the impression of a vibrato taking place about a note slightly higher than the original note.

In the following passage (theme from the film: "The Third Man") the 1st, 2nd, and 3rd strings are plucked by the middle, index finger and thumb respectively. Vibrato is used to help imitate the sound of the zither.

Exercise 36

False vibrato is perfectly acceptable in most instances and is the only option available for vibrato when plucking all three strings together. Pressing down on the bridge (using the "true" vibrato method) would deaden the 2nd and 3rd strings.

*Photo:*
*In false vibrato, the note is raised above its true pitch by intermittent pressure applied by the heel of the right hand to the A-string beyond the bridge.*

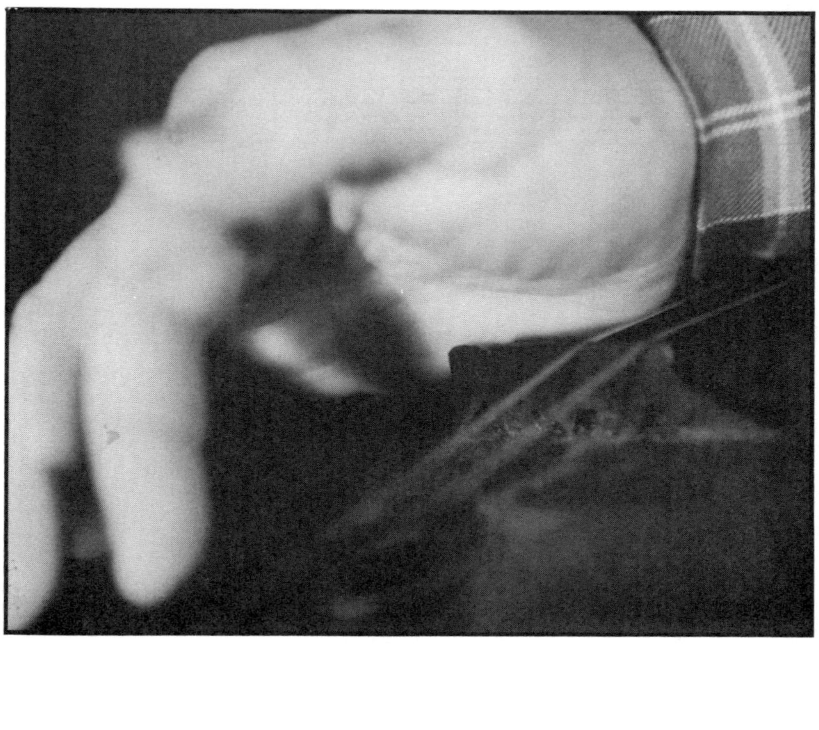

When playing vibrato, the right-hand index finger plucks the string upwards with a stroking movement along its length, producing a warm, soft, delicate sound. Another interesting sound is produced by playing all three strings simultaneously in just the same way, stroking them upwards with the index finger while vibrating all three strings beyond the bridge with the heel of the hand.

Plucking with the middle instead of index finger produces a slightly harsher sound; plucking with either finger near the bridge produces a harder, shorter sound.

Pizzicato vibrato, as this style of playing is called, sounds effective when used sparingly and appropriately, especially as it contrasts so vividly with a regular three string tremolo.

Pizzicato vibrato is most often used on the steel "A" string for slow single-string variations, where the emotional quality of the passage is heightened by being played in this manner rather than "straight."

Occasionally, vibrato will be used for faster passages when, due to the tiring effect it has, the index and middle fingers may both be used to alternately pluck the same string. Vibrato is also effective when used with "Guitar Picking." (See section on Guitar Techniques.)

Vibrato helps sustain the note longer and is often used with harmonics.

Exercise 37

"Suburban Moscow Evenings" - (Solovyev-Sedoi)

**Vibrato on the 2nd string** is produced by the left hand with the finger not only pressing down the string, but also moving it quickly from side to side across the fret. Because of the short ring of nylon strings, this stroke is not very effective.

Exercise 38

"Two Guitars" (Dvie Gitary) - *Russian Gypsy song*

arr.: Bibs Ekkel

# Tremolo With Vibrato

For tremolo with vibrato on one string the heel of the right hand is used as described for vibrato. (See preceding section.) The index finger, supported by the thumb, tremoloes the string as part of the vibrato movement, while the remaining fingers may brush the scratchplate to facilitate evenness.

*In the upper register, tremolo-vibrato can be used to imitate a violin quite effectively.*

Tremolo-vibrato may be used on all three strings together. This requires the index finger to be bent and held stiffly without support, while the remaining fingers on the one side and the thumb on the other stick out to provide a counterbalance.

Tremolo-vibrato on all strings can only be used for very quiet passages as it is not very loud.

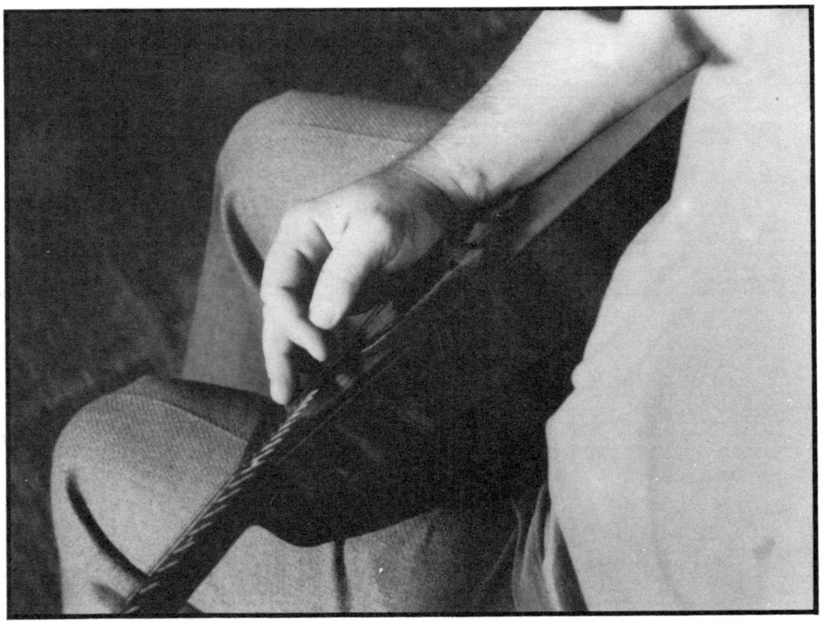

Exercise 39

Csardas: Monti (excerpt) – arr. Bibs Ekkel

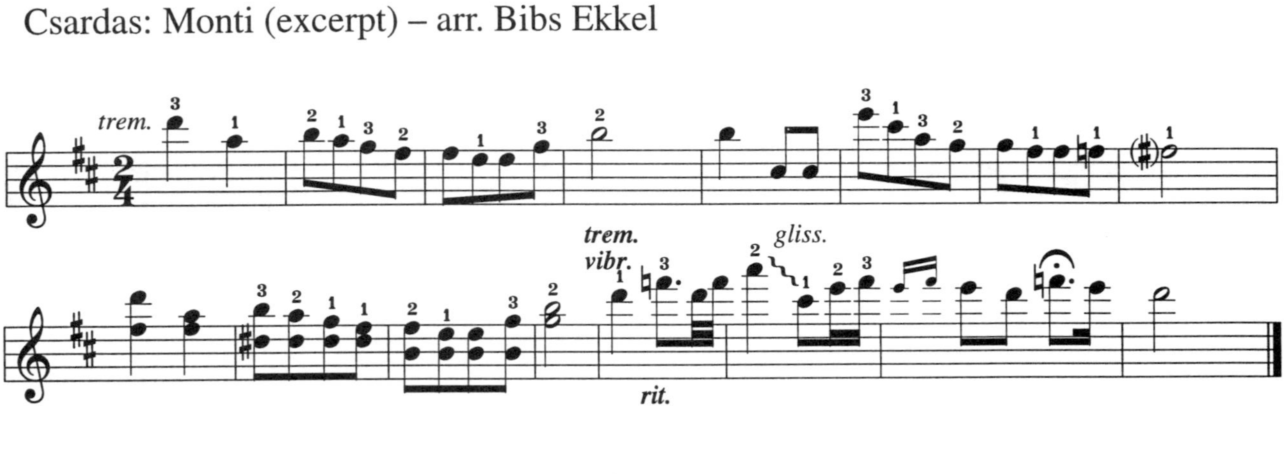

## Compare the following:

Exercise 40

Tremolo-Vibrato on one string:

and on all strings:

from "Willow Tree" - Ponomarenko

# Rolls

The fingers of the right hand are bunched up as shown, with the thumb touching the little finger. The hand faces sideways towards the head of the balalaika (not downwards). With the wrist bent (though not loose), the hand is poised above the strings so that the top joint of the little finger is above the 3rd string. The fingers are stiffened and released by the thumb one by one in quick succession, starting with the little finger. As they are released, each finger strikes all three strings sideways, to be closely followed by the next finger – providing a continuous flowing sound. At the same time, the hand and forearm move slightly downward, facilitating the smooth execution of the roll.

In the ***Large Roll***, the downward movement of the hand and forearm is far more pronounced, as the thumb is the last digit to strike the string and the whole hand ends up near the bottom of the scratchplate. (See photos below.)

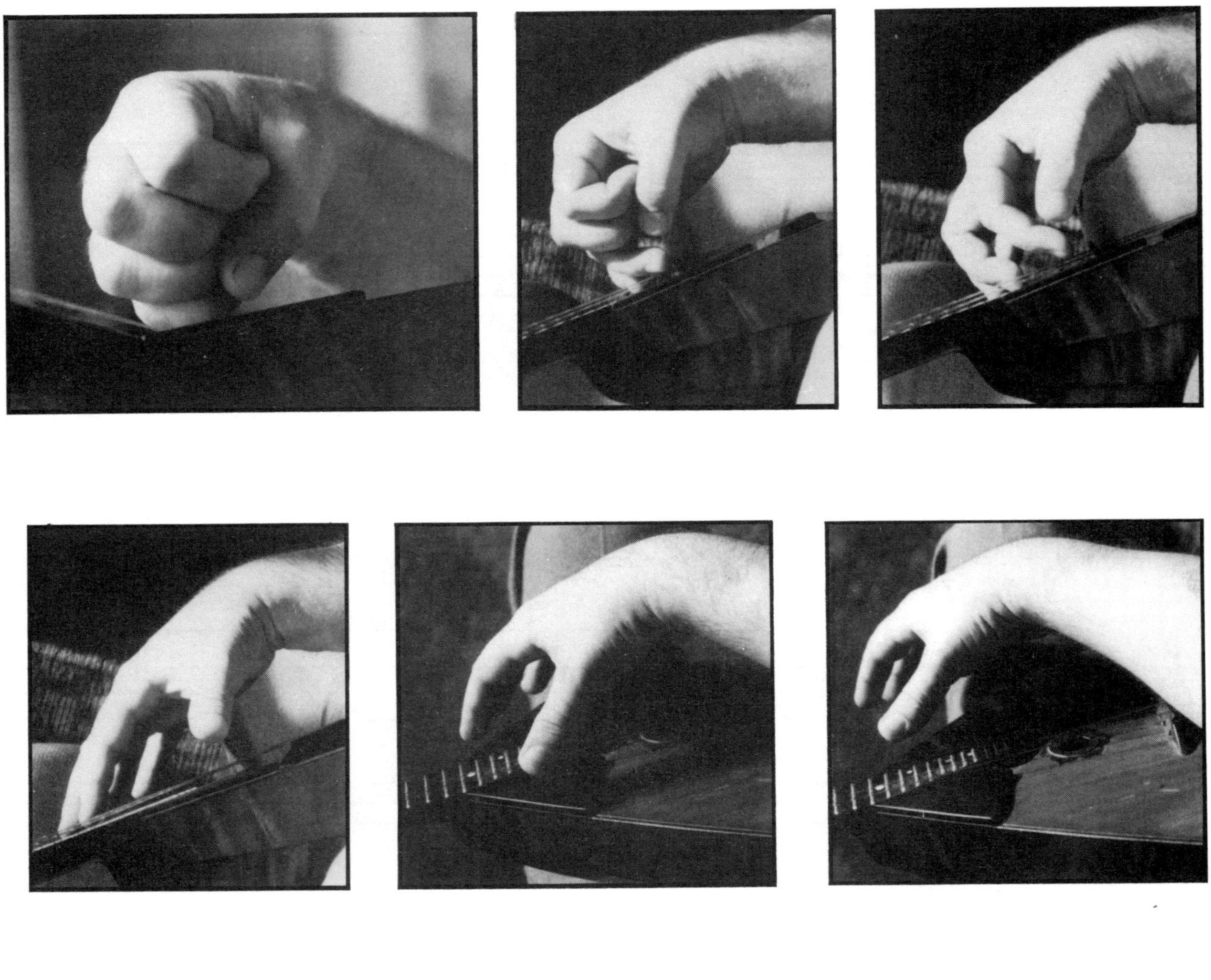

Large rolls in this tutor are indicated with a double wavy line and sometimes **б. др.** (the Russian "b" for bolshoi, meaning "large") above the chord. This is only one of a number of ways large rolls are commonly indicated. Quite often a single wavy line is used with a thumb marked above it.

sometimes written:

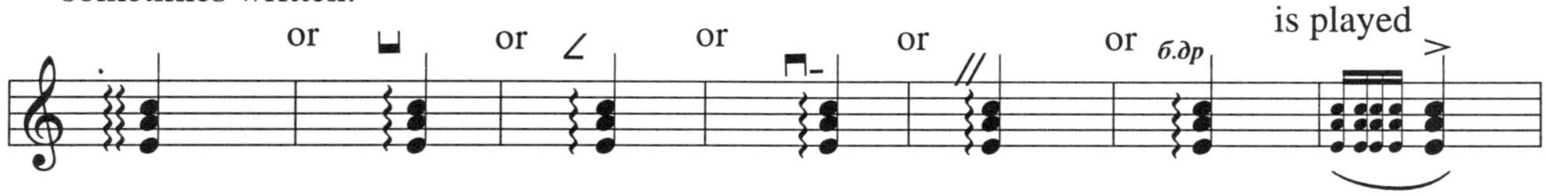


Rolls are commonly used for the first chord of pieces or sections played with rhythmic strumming, where they serve to further underline the accent on the first beat.

Exercise 41

Exercise 42

Exercise 43

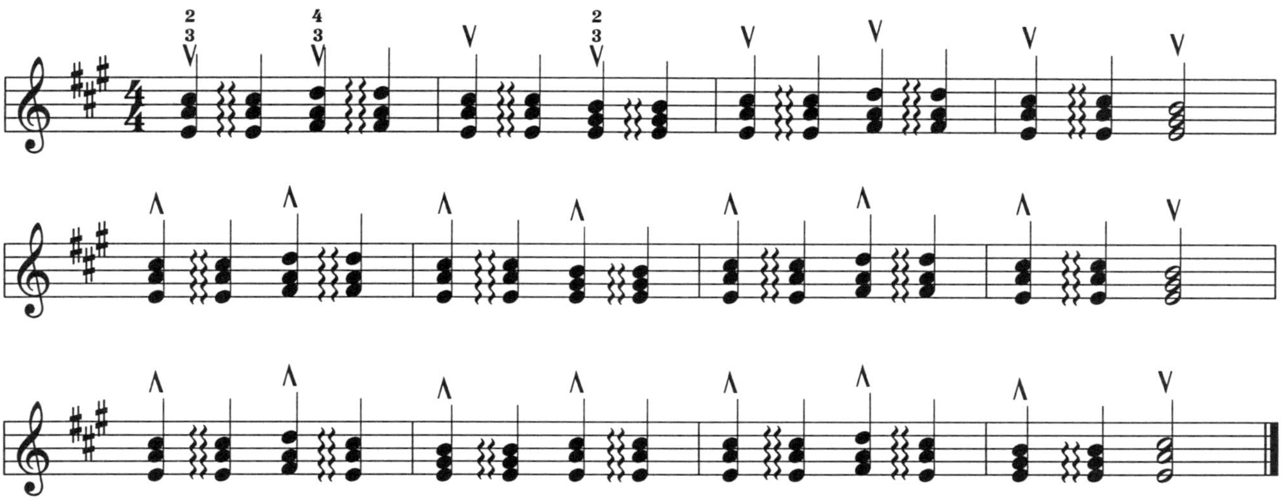

In the ***Small Roll*** (so called because no thumb is involved), the index finger is the last finger to strike the strings, and the thumb is lifted outward to avoid hitting the 3rd string.[1]

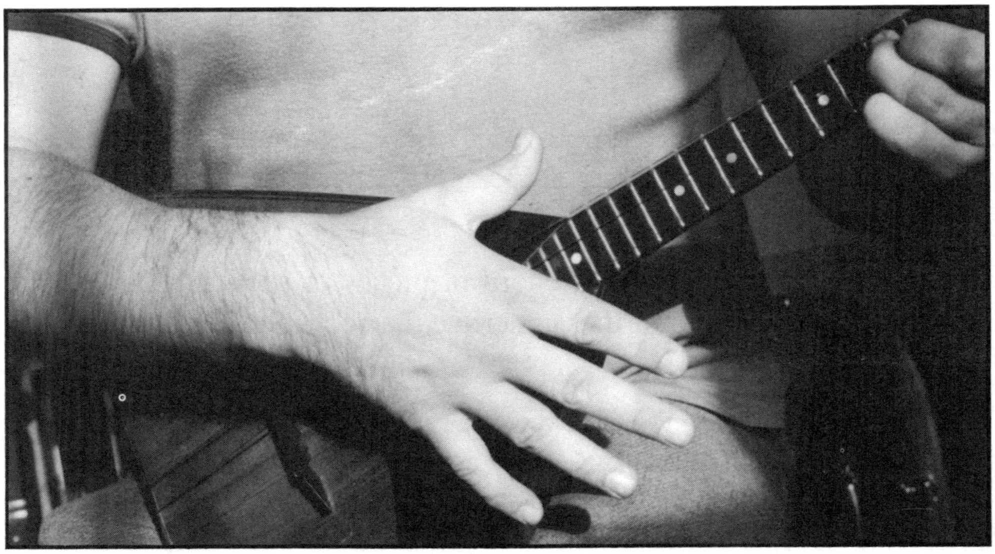

The small roll is normally indicated by a wavy perpendicular line before the chord, the same as for arpeggiato, but with a downward pointing arrow above it. Often, however, the Russian letters **др.** (*∂p.*) or **м. др.** are added above the chord to indicate a small roll. In these cases the wavy line is sometimes omitted.

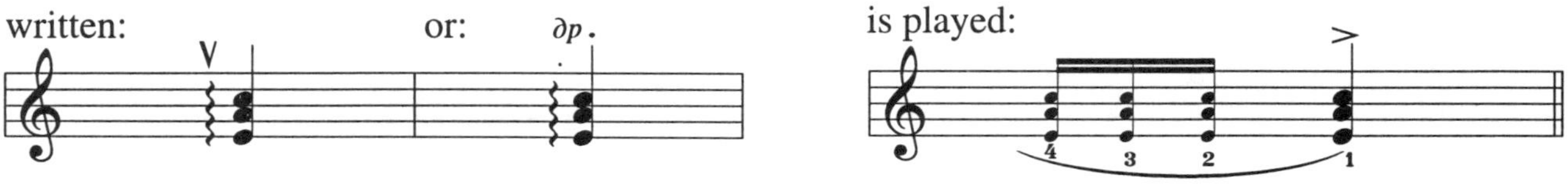


Very often the chord following a small roll is played by a separate stroke downward with the thumb after a small delay. In this case, the fingers brush the strings in turn as described previously, but as they do so the thumb is flung sharply upwards, the elbow lifted and the hand moved slightly forward as part of a semi-circular movement, which ends in the thumb being brought down to strum the strings. The forward movement of the forearm facilitates the delay of this second beat and makes this technique especially useful where the second beat played with the thumb is accentuated.

Exercise 44

[1] Due to the absence of a unified system of balalaika notation, there are several different ways of indicating rolls. Here, as always in this tutor, the author has opted for the self-explanatory 'arrow' system (as espoused, among others, by the St. Petersburg Conservatoire).

In the ***Upward Roll*** (shown below), the hand is held pointing sideways (nails facing towards the head of the instrument) and the fingers are brushed upwards one by one across the strings starting with the index finger and ending with the little finger.

Sometimes, instead of the conventional wavy line with upward-pointing arrow, the letters **обр. др.** are used above the chord to indicate an **upward roll**.

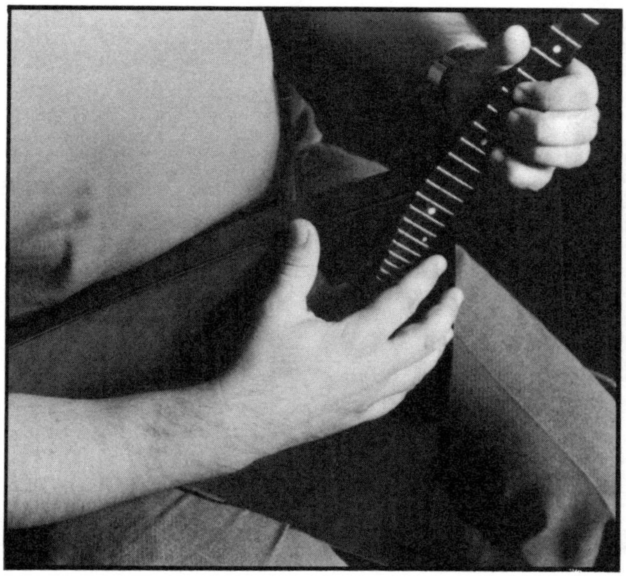

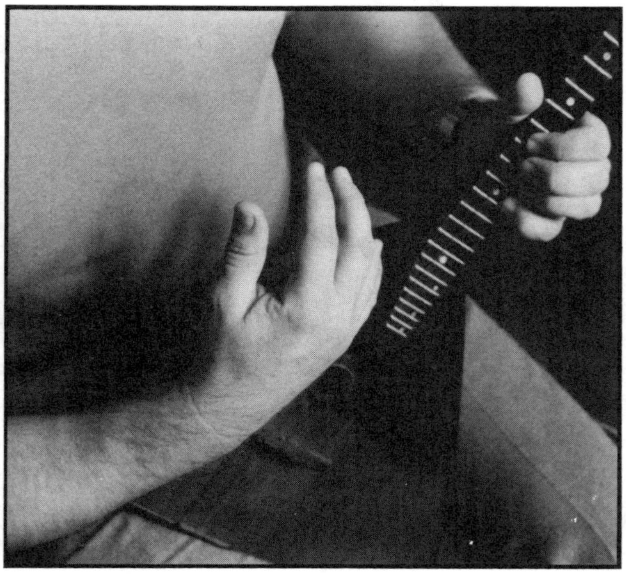

Ending an upward roll with the 3rd finger (rather than the 4th) can be used to add clarity to the individual notes struck, or to create a specific rhythm.

Exercise 45

***Compare:***

***and:***

(Also see the section on Syncopation).

"Under the Apple Tree" (Kak pod yablonkoy) - *Russian folk melody*

# SYNCOPATION

A series of strokes with the index finger and thumb may alternate with a roll in a particular sequence, forming a rhythmic pattern in which particular chords are emphasized.

Exercise 46

*In these examples 'reminder' RH markings have been added:* R = roll
T = downstroke with thumb
Accentuated chords are marked: >

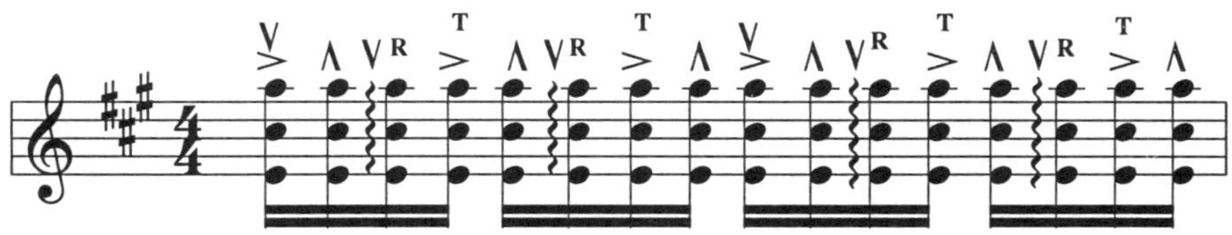

Exercise 47

"I Stroll Around Moscow" (excerpt) by A. Petrov arr. M. Rozhkov

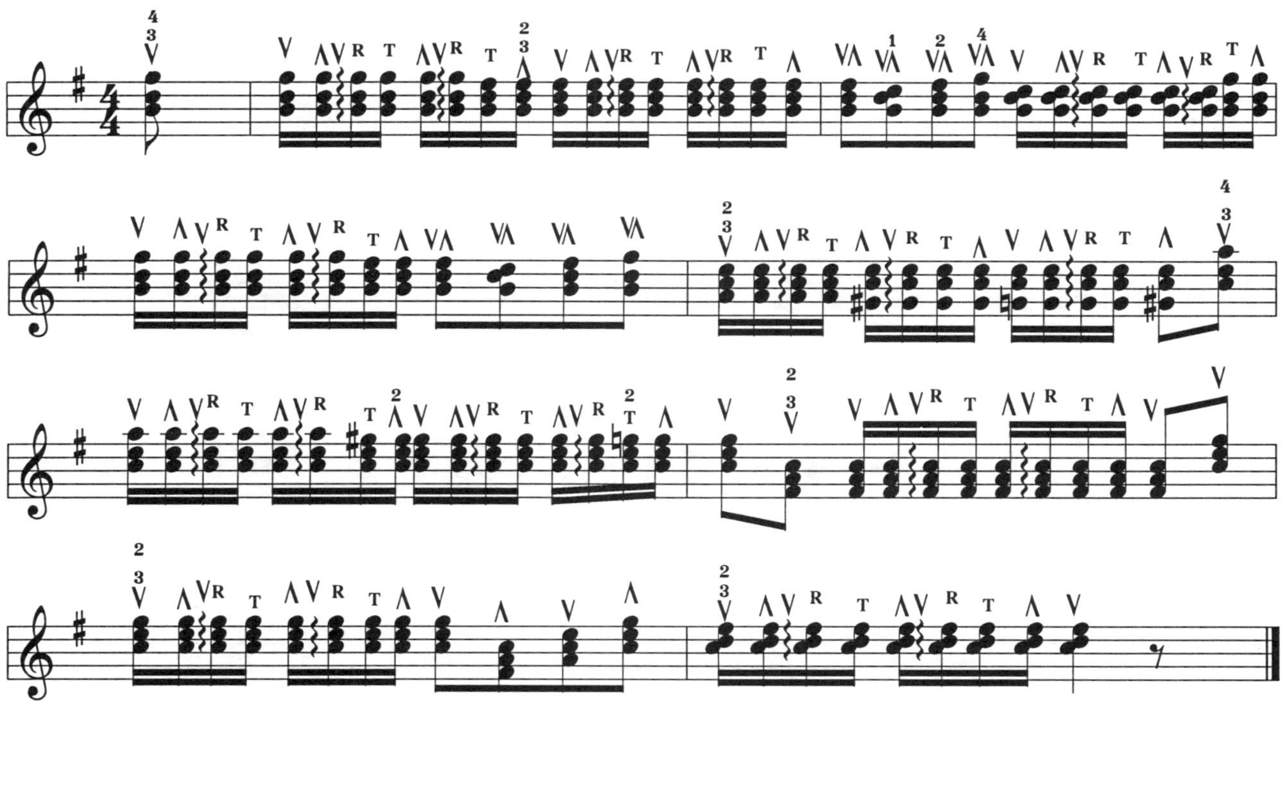

***Another interesting technique is to use a down-stroke with the index finger in place of the small (downward) roll. Try the same examples again this way.***

An upward roll may also be used in similar configurations, particularly when a "Spanish" effect is required.

Exercise 48

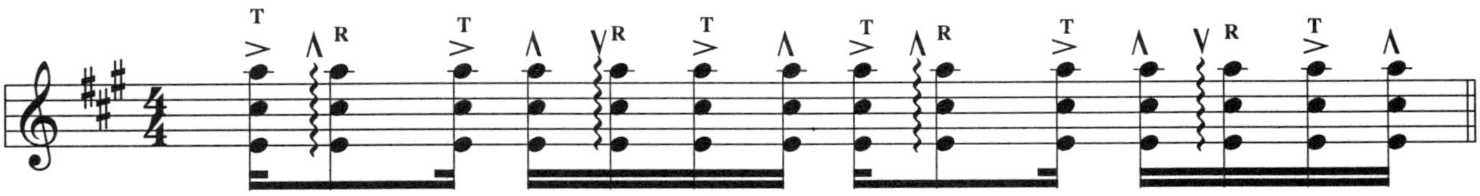

Be sure to strongly accent the chords where marked >
Note that upward rolls tend to be more drawn-out, downward ones more brief.

Exercise 49

Written:

May in effect be played:

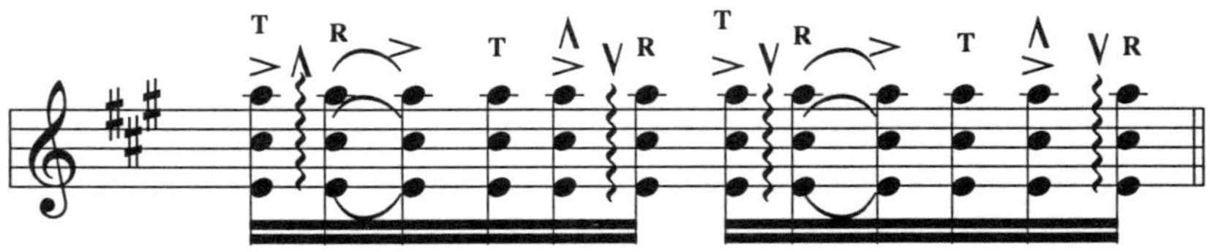

Exercise 50

"Lady of Spain"

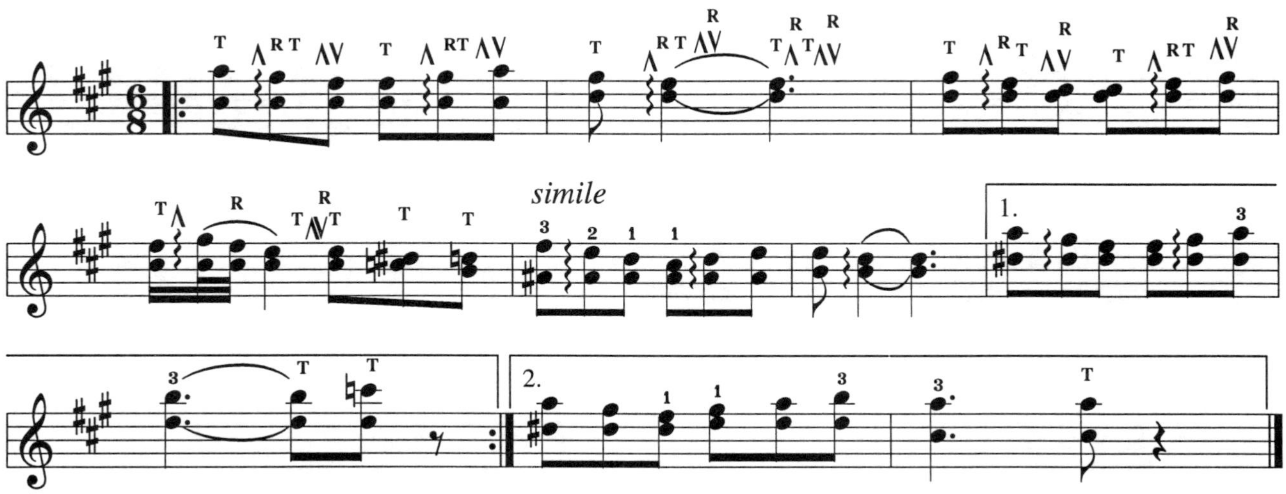


NOTE: An alternative way of playing an upward roll can be used (similar to "straight-fingered guitar pizzicato" - *see p. 64)* whereby fingers 4, 3, 2, & 1 successively brush the strings upwards and towards the bridge.

# Left-hand Pizzicato

(Pulling Off and Hammering On) *(Marked + above or below a note)*

**Pulling Off** involves plucking the string with a finger of the left hand (without any use of the right hand). A finger in place on the fingerboard, pressing down a string in the usual manner, is pulled sideways off the string in such a way that in doing so it plucks it, thus sounding the note already being held below by the next finger.

The right hand is often used to pluck the first of a series of such notes to be plucked with the left hand only.

Exercise 51

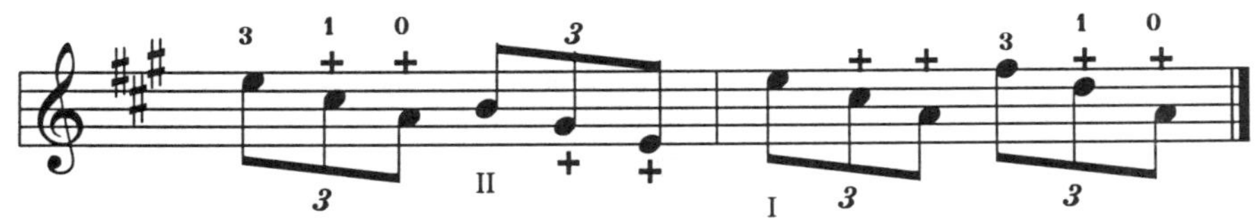

Exercise 52

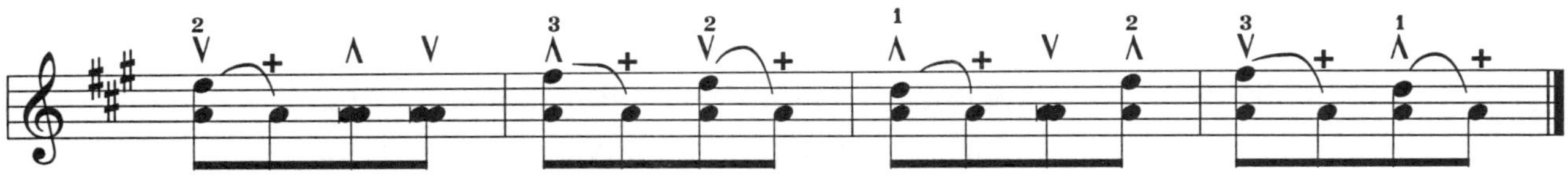

Exercise 53

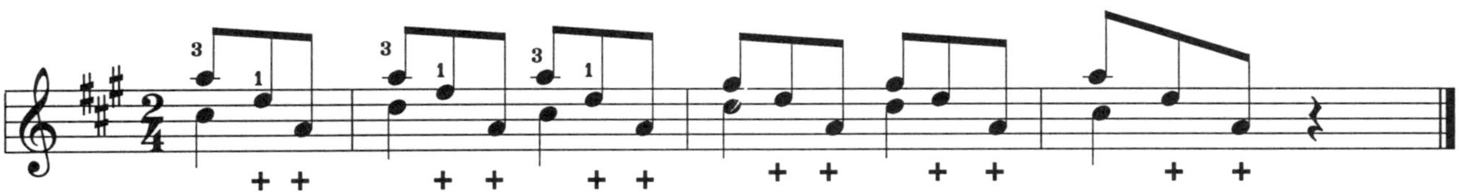

Exercise 54

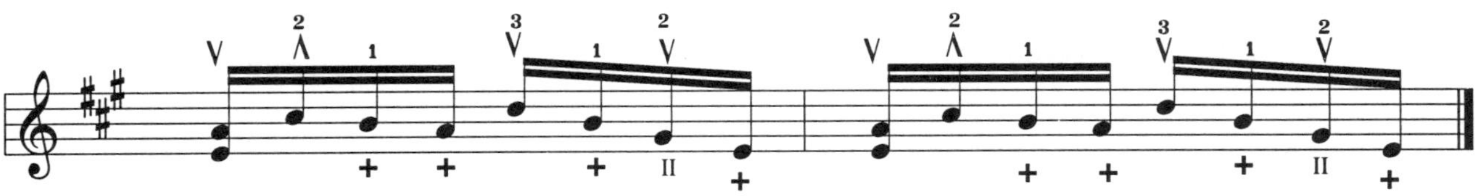

*If the top string has been set too near the edge of the fingerboard, it will tend to slip over the side as the finger is pulled sideways, thus making this technique difficult.*

The left-hand thumb can be used to pluck the third string (viz).

Exercise 55

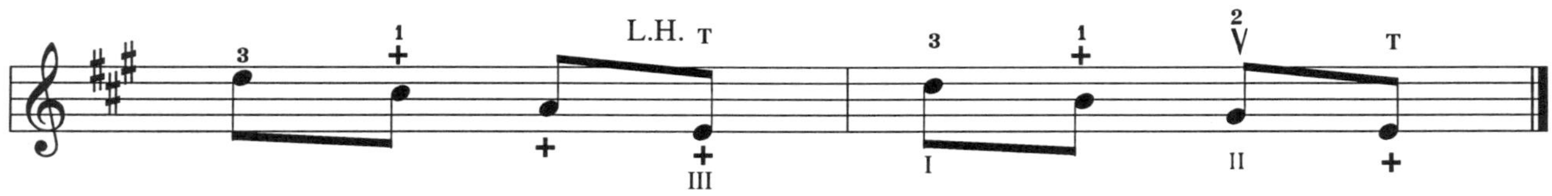


Exercise 56

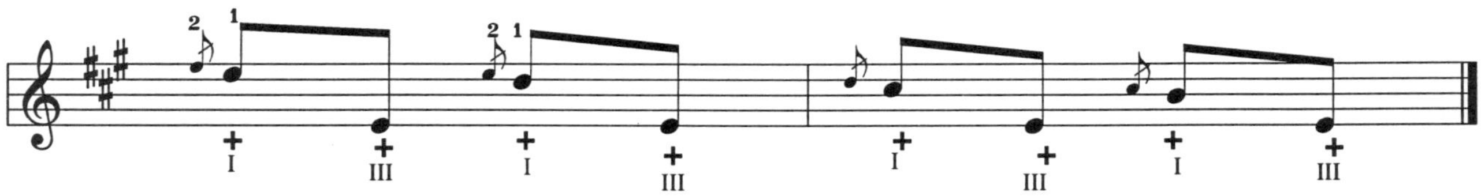


**Hammering On** *(likewise marked + above or below a note)* is another method of sounding the strings with the left hand only, and the one used for playing notes in an upward progression. For the note to sound at all loudly, it is necessary for the finger to hammer down onto the string as perpendicularly and as hard as possible. The fingers will need to be lifted high and to strike the string at just the right spot behind the fret, using the metal fret as an anvil.

With a combination of left-hand pizzicato for the descending notes, and "hammering on" with the left hand for the ascending notes, it is possible to play even quite long passages without the assistance of the right hand.

Practice will be needed to get notes in a mixed passage of hammering on and pulling off to sound with equal volume.

*(For extra clarity, the hammered notes in these two examples have been marked with an (H).)*

Exercise 57

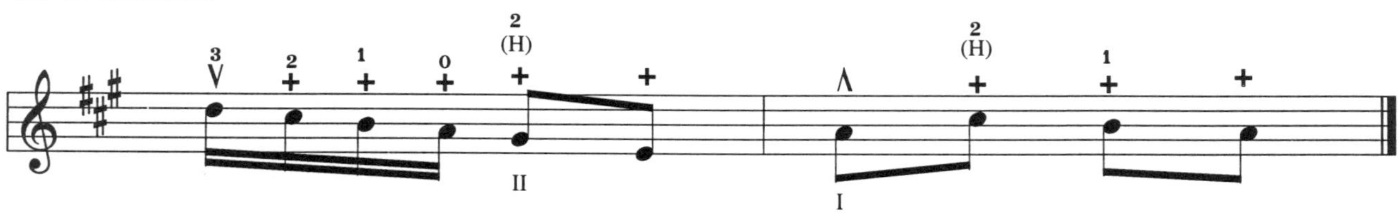


Exercise 58

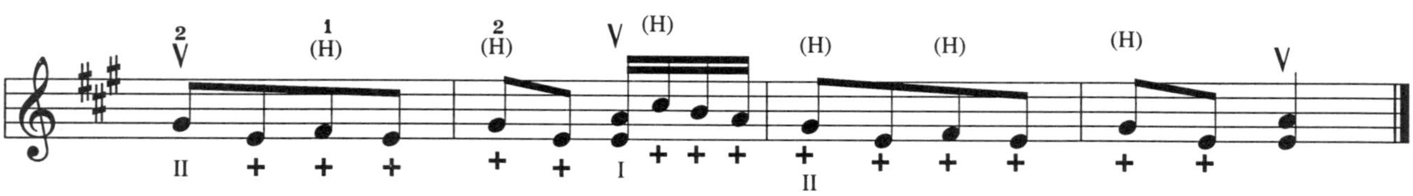


*(Usually, however, notes whether hammered or pulled off are marked identically with just a +)*

Kamarinskaya - After B. Feoktistov - *Traditional Russian Melody*

Exercise 60

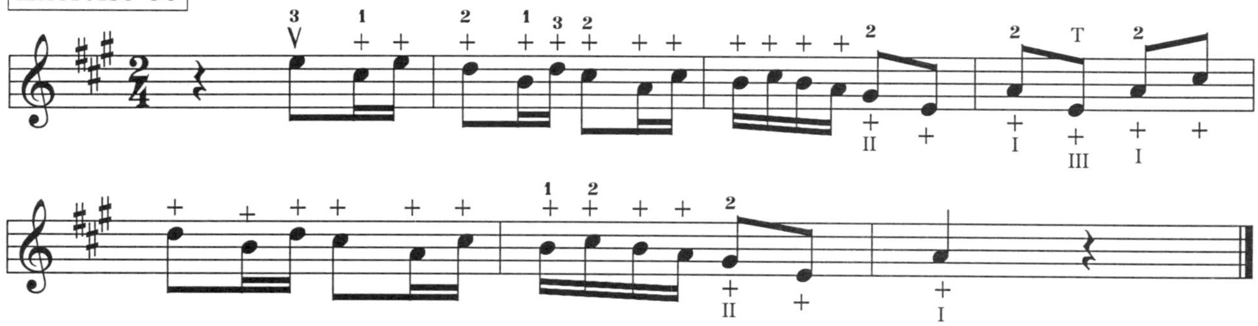

Such passages can be used to display the player's dexterity (e.g. raising the right hand in the air with a flourish where only the left hand is playing) - *see section on tricks and special effects*. However, an important use of this technique is to provide a particular tonal effect.

Exercise 61

Left-hand pizzicato is commonly used for sounding the second of two slurred notes.

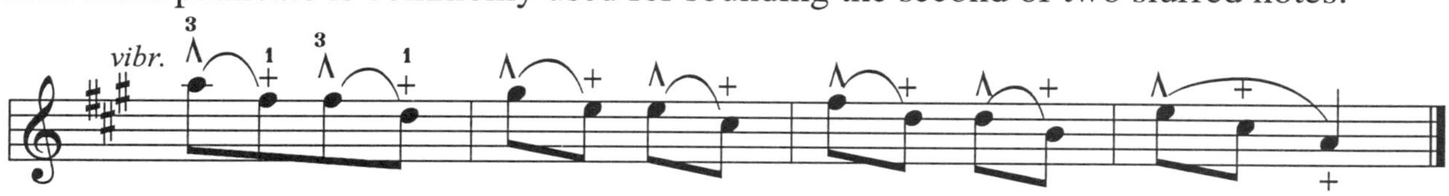


Exercise 62

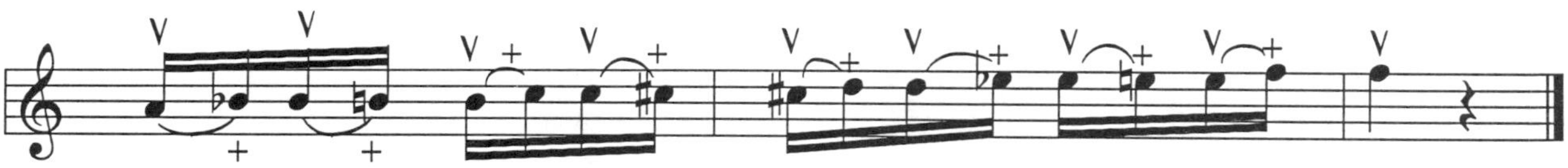

***Play the above passage through again using vibrato (up-strokes instead of down). Note the differences in the sound produced.***

Waltz No. 1 - Durand (excerpt)

# GLISSANDO

**Glissando** (sliding) is when the left hand is slid from one position to another while pressing the string or strings. The right hand may be required to either pluck the strings once at the beginning of the slide or tremolo them very fast continuously, so that not only the first and last notes are sounded but the intermediate ones as well.

Glissando is written as a wavy line joining the first and last notes or chords of the slide.

Very often the abbreviation *"gliss."* is added.

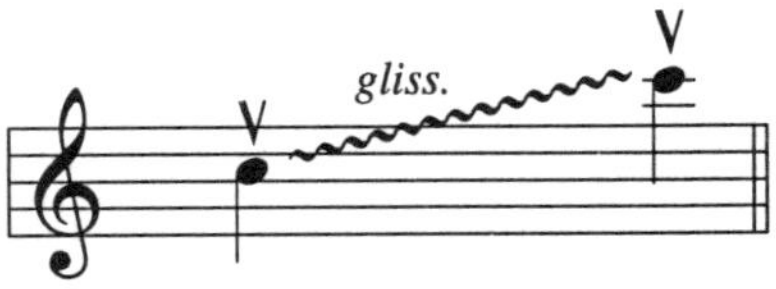


Exercise 63

Exercise 64

In the following example you slide with one finger and hammer with the adjacent finger.

Exercise 65

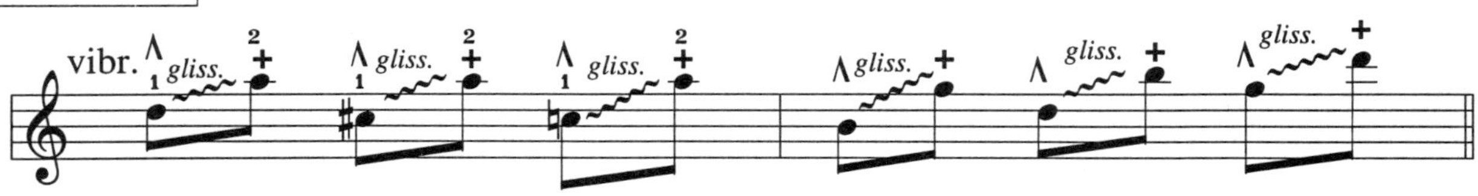


One of the hardest things for beginners to master is glissando when playing tremolo on all three strings. The friction created by the hand gripping the neck along with the fingers and thumb pressing the strings against the frets impedes the hand's even progress along the neck, thereby spoiling the effect. Hardest of all is a descending glissando, which requires extra bodily effort to hold the instrument in place because the left hand tends to pull the instrument out of its normally held position.

Exercise 66

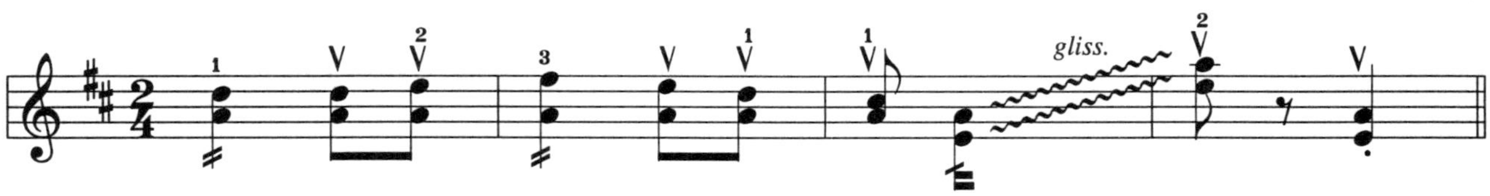

***Practice the following:***

Exercise 67

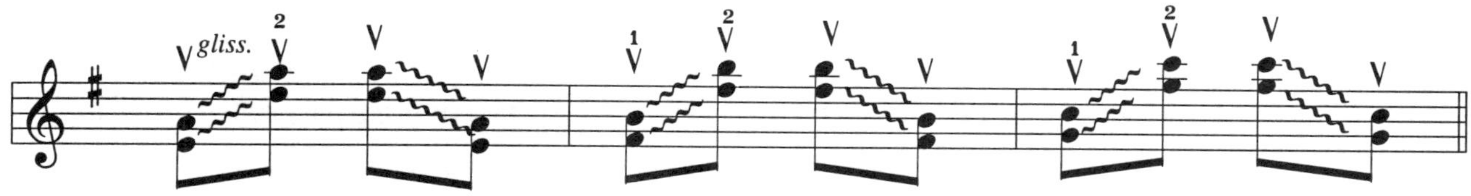


Exercise 68

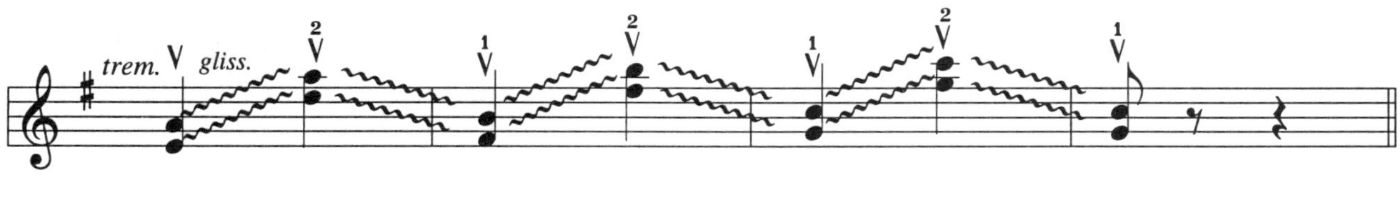


"I Went Up A Hill" (Ya Na Gorku Shla) - *Russian Folk Song*

# Harmonics

(Flagolettes)

Players of other stringed instruments will be familiar with these already. By lightly touching (not pressing down) a string immediately above the 12th fret with the tip of one of the fingers of the left hand and breaking this contact just as the string is plucked, one can produce a harmonic – a light ringing sound of the same pitch as the note produced by pressing the string at the 12th fret (i.e. one octave above the open string).

With practice the quality of the harmonic can be improved: the accompanying thud as the string is plucked lessened, and the actual harmonic made louder.

*Seen here: the middle finger plays the harmonic*

Exercise 69

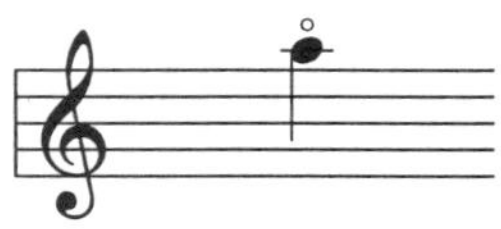

Other harmonics will be produced in a similar manner at the 19th or 24th frets and identical notes to these at the 7th and 5th frets respectively.

These natural or "true" harmonics are usually written with a little circle above the note produced (see above).
Another way they may be written is thus: Exercise 70

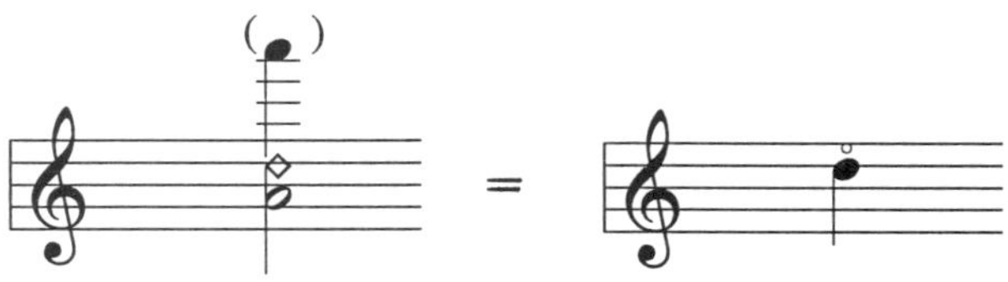

At 5th fret.

Here a diamond shape shows the fret above which the string is touched, while the normal note as written shows where the string is pressed by the left hand (in this case an open string). The resulting note produced is sometimes added in brackets above.

This method of notation is regularly used for "false" harmonics.

Natural harmonics are found at points which divide the string into 1/2, 1/3, and 1/4

Exercise 71

| | | | | | | |
|---|---|---|---|---|---|---|
| Division: | 1/2 | | 1/3 | | 1/4 | |
| String: | E | A | E | A | E | A |
| Fret: | 12 | 12 | 7&19 | 7&19 | 5&24 | 5&24 |

Other, much fainter harmonics occur where the string is divided into 1/5, 1/6, and 1/8. These are best produced near the bridge and much precision is needed for the thud of the string being plucked not to drown out the harmonic altogether. Also with no frets to act as a visual guide, the player will have to memorize the exact spots where these high harmonics occur.

Exercise 72

# False Harmonics

The word "false" here provides a convenient distinction between these and naturally occurring (true) harmonics where the string is not pressed down with the left hand.

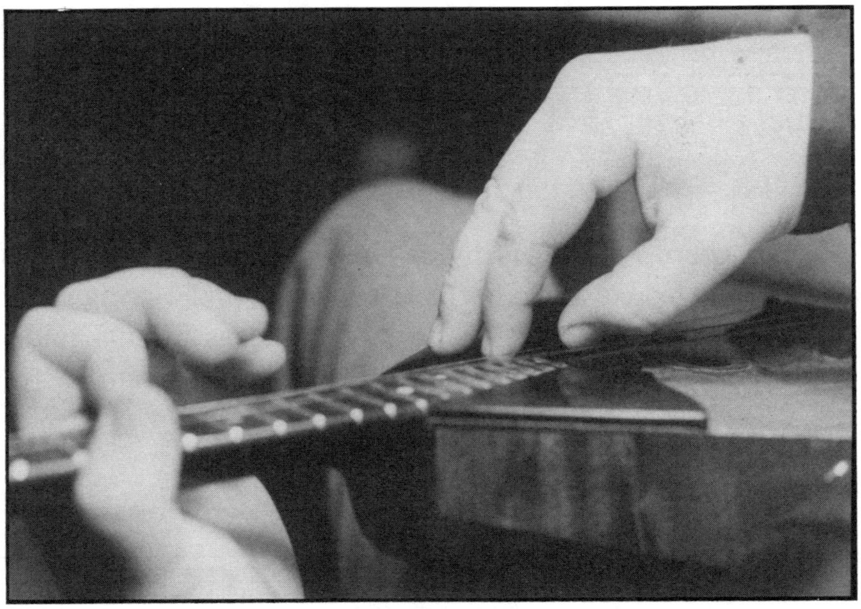

***Shown Here:***
*The A-String is pressed at the 10th fret. The R.H. thumb plucks the string while the index finger produces the harmonic above the 22nd fret.*

For the production of false harmonics the loudest harmonic points of the string are normally used (i.e.: where the string is divided into half, a third and a quarter). False harmonics are harder to play, being produced by the right hand alone, and as a result are usually not as loud as natural ones.

The fingers of the left hand press the string to the particular fret in question: thus establishing the base note. The right hand is held as shown, with the index finger selecting the position of the harmonic on the string. The top joint of the index finger is laid sideways against the string, touching it lightly. The right-hand thumb plucks the string downwards against the index finger, which draws away at the moment of plucking, thus producing the harmonic.

The position of harmonics occurring naturally at the 5th, 7th, 12th, 19th, and 24th frets will now be raised by the number of frets pressed down in this way.

Thus, if the string is pressed at the 2nd fret, harmonics will be found above the 7th, 9th, 14th, 21st, and 26th (if you have one) frets. With this method, a harmonic can be produced of any note within the balalaika's range.

*The lower notes show the fret pressed; the diamond shape above indicates the point at which the string is touched.*

Exercise 73

From Waltz No. 1 by Durand (arr. B. Ekkel)

N.B. Harmonics are useful for checking that the bridge is correctly positioned. The note played at the 12th fret should be the same as the harmonic produced at the same point.

Vibrato will prolong the sound of the harmonic and will add to its effectiveness.

# TRIADS

Difficulties with fingering sometimes occur when playing three note chords (triads). This is especially true when playing legato and where lifting a finger to change it from one string to another would interrupt the tremolo. The correct fingering, therefore, must be carefully chosen. The thumb almost invariably plays the lowest note of each triad and therefore may often not be indicated in the fingering.

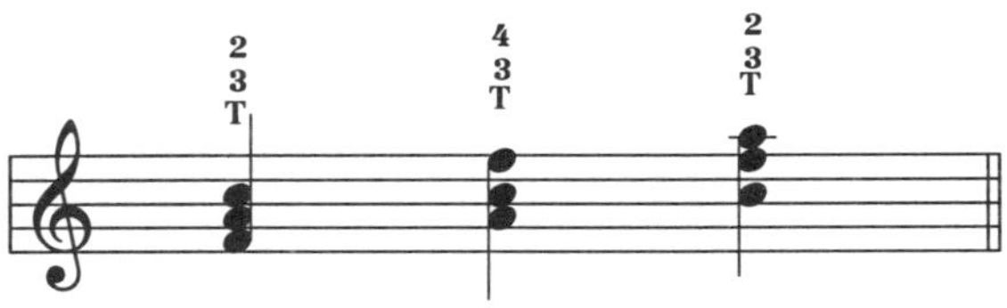

Exercise 74

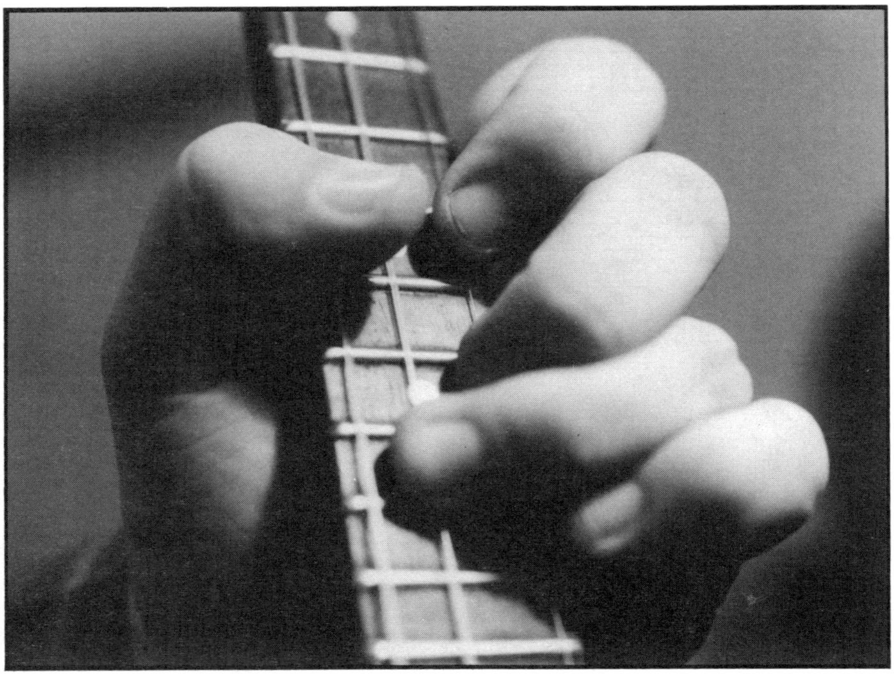

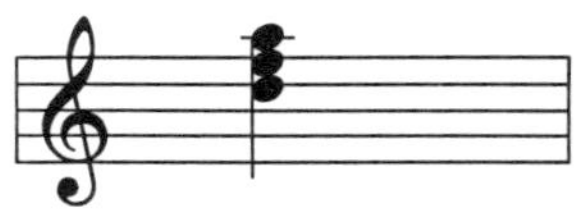

Exercise 75

In Exercise 75 either the 2nd or 3rd string may be left open.

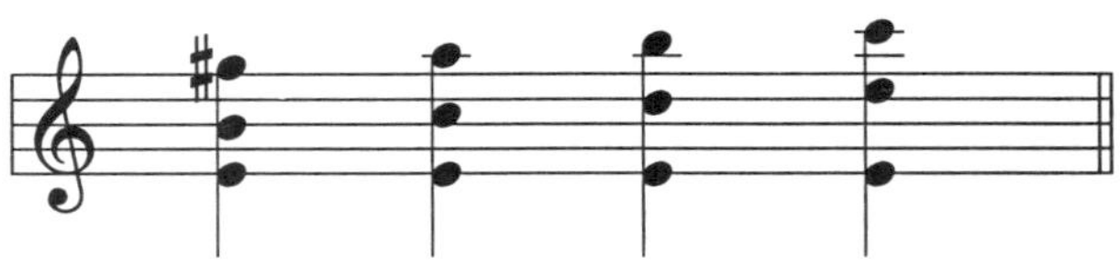

# "Guitar" Techniques

Over the last few years the term "Guitar techniques" or "Guitar strokes" (**гитарные приемы** - *gitarniye priyomy*) has become accepted as collectively defining two important and difficult balalaika strokes: "guitar tremolo" and "guitar pizzicato" and a third, easier one called "guitar picking" (**гитарный перебор** - *gitarnyi perebor*).

While "Guitar tremolo" and "picking" might indeed be borrowed techniques, being different for the balalaika in not using wrist and forearm movement, "Guitar pizzicato" presumably acquired its "guitar" connotation due to its superficial similarity to Rasquando, whereby the guitar is strummed across all strings in turn with four stiffened fingers. In the case of the balalaika, the stroke is not a strum but rather a pizzicato on the top string only (usually for playing grace notes or short fast runs of up to five notes).

Even if not strictly accurate, "guitar technique" is a term of convenience, and in the absence of a more appropriate classification has become generally accepted (as has the technique itself). Relatively unknown thirty years ago, today "guitar techniques" are widely used and are considered standard skills in the arsenal of any self-respecting balalaika player.

## "Guitar" Tremolo

A technique widely used for the guitar in which the thumb plucks the 2nd or 3rd string downward, following which the 3rd, 2nd, and 1st fingers consecutively pluck the top string, curling upwards towards the palm. At speed a tremolo effect is produced on the top string.

In this technique the fingers are held half-curled just below the top string. The wrist and forearm play a passive role, angling the hand in a comfortable, relaxed position allowing the fingers and thumb total freedom.

Although a high speed can be achieved using this energy-efficient technique, one disadvantage is the limited volume that it can produce. Most passages can be played much louder, if necessary, and with more control over individual notes, by using the physically more taxing double pizzicato.

***Make sure the melody string ( I ) remains louder than the accompanying ones (II & III).***

Exercise 76

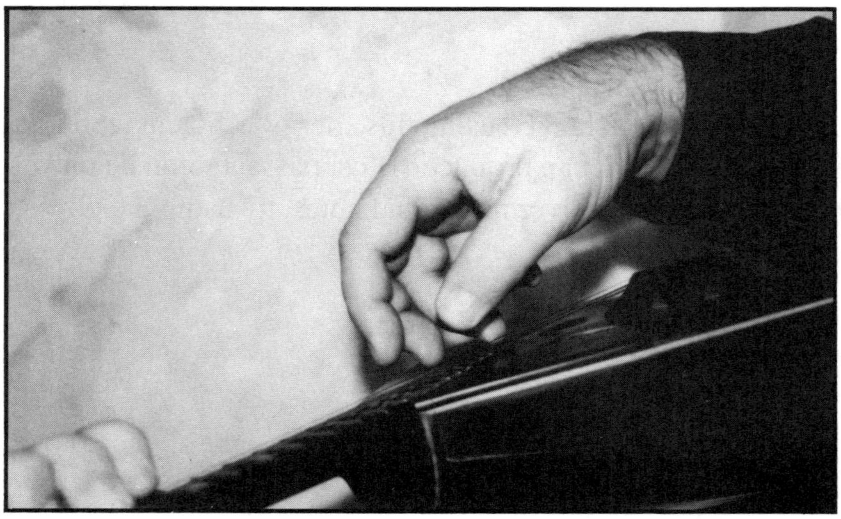

## "Guitar" Pizzicato ( Г-pizz./Г-пицц.)

*Usually used for short and fast pizzicato passages, grace notes, or trills involving up to five notes.*

There is more than one way this stroke may be played. The first and arguably most widespread method stems from – and is played similarly to – Guitar tremolo. The only basic difference being that whereas the tremolo is played by fingers 3, 2 and 1, guitar pizzicato sometimes involves the fourth (little) finger as well.[1]

***Play the following examples. Note that with guitar pizzicato the order of the R.H. fingers is normally indicated beneath the staff.***

Exercise 77

*Guitar pizzicato is best mastered by first practicing on an open string.*

Exercise 78

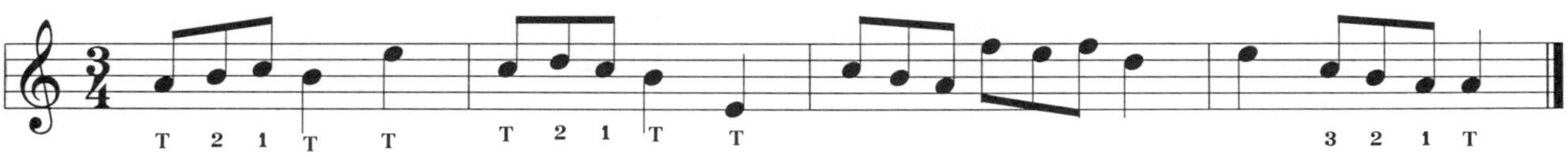


Exercise 79

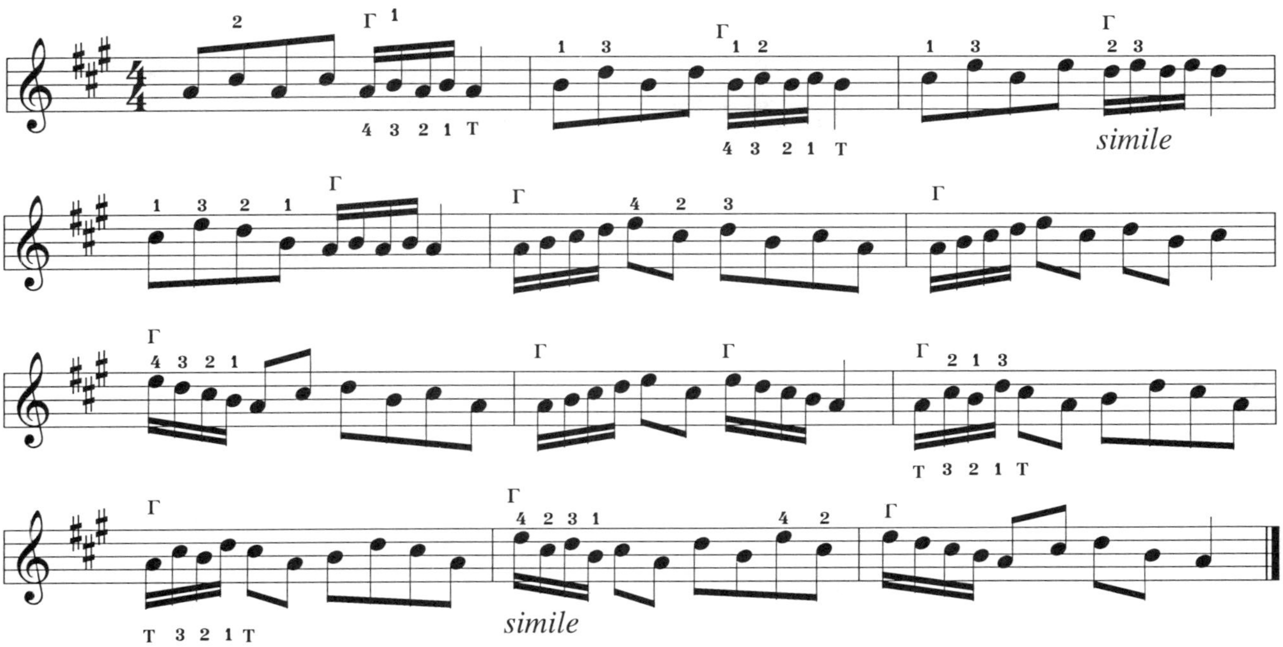


[1] This is the "guitar pizzicato" technique (using curled fingers in the order 4, 3, 2, 1, T), most favored and propagated by Prof. Pavel Necheporenko and his many students at the Gnessin Academy of Music in Moscow.

## Forward Guitar Pizzicato *(Recommended)*

Like the preceding method, this is another curled-fingered pizzicato, but one in which the order of the fingers is reversed. The thumb first plays a down-stroke followed by upward strokes from the curled index, middle, and 3rd finger and ending with a down-stroke from the thumb.[1] Here the little finger is limited to acting as a guide for the hand, brushing the scratchplate.

*With the hand held horizontally, the fingers curl upward to pluck the string in front of the thumb and the forearm moves to assist the stroke.*

Exercise 80

***Practice all the preceding and following examples using this stroke.***

Exercise 81

[1] Technique favored by balalaika virtuoso Mikhail Rozhkov.

Exercise 82

When four notes are played in a series (using the above method), the last note may be played with the thumb or third finger as required (T, 1, 2, 3, or T, 1, 2, T). Also, the first note of a series may be played not with the thumb, but the index finger (1, 2, 3, T or 1, 2, T). Each means provides a different tone– use of the thumb allowing a heavier stress on a note or chord to be applied.

Exercise 83

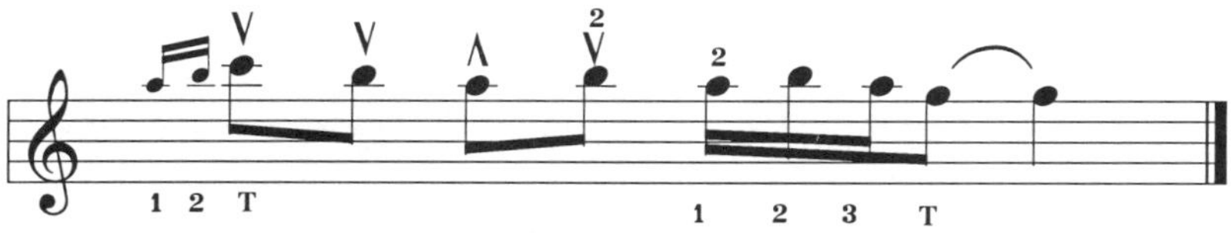

Exercise 84

Exercise 85

**Trills**

Written:

Played:

## Straight-Fingered Guitar Pizzicato

The fingers of the right hand are stiffened and spread apart. Starting with the little finger (when five notes are to be played) and followed by the 3rd, 2nd, and 1st, the fingers swing round towards the bridge, plucking the A-string sideways from below. The notes are struck evenly, one after another, and finish with a down-stroke from the thumb.

The elbow is lifted slightly during the stroke which ends with a downward movement of the forearm when the thumb plays the final note (or chord).

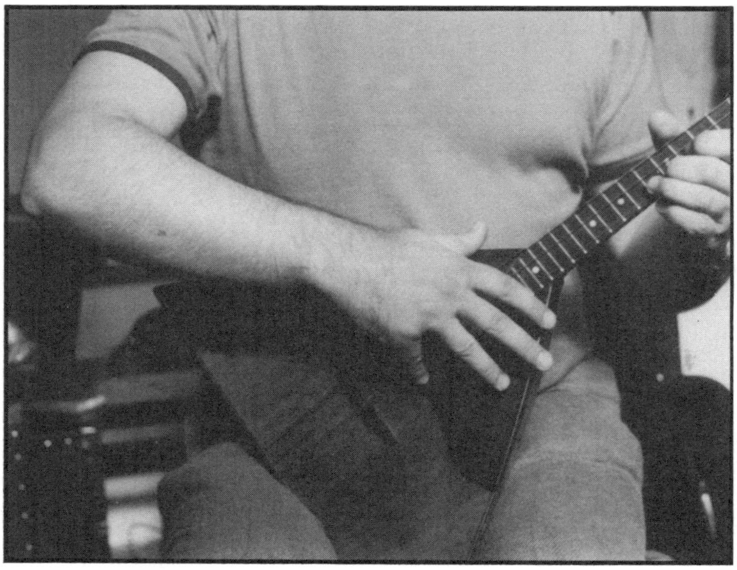

# Bibs Ekkel: Complete Balalaika



Exercise 86

When playing a run of four notes, the first note is played with the 3rd (ring) finger, not the 4th.

Exercise 87

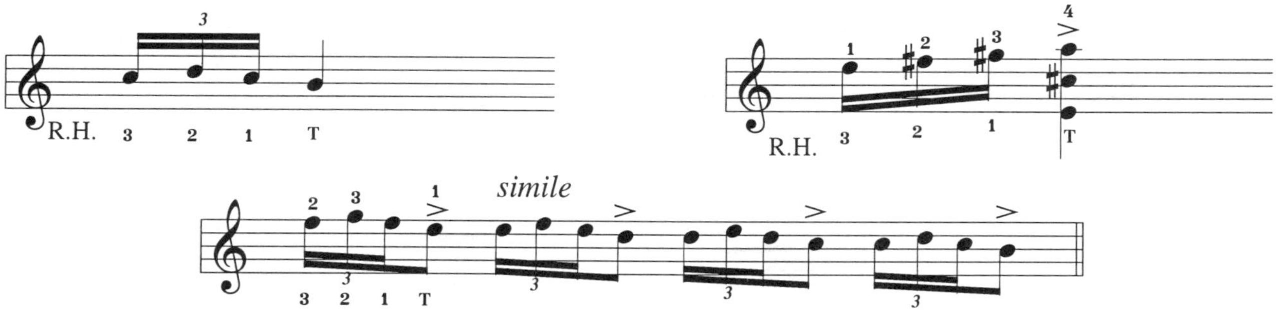


In the following example Γ = guitar stroke

*After playing Ex. 88 through as indicated, try again, this time using alternative strokes – as described in this section.*

Exercise 88

## Guitar Picking

This involves the R.H. thumb, index and middle finger plucking the III, II and I strings respectively. There is no wrist or forearm movement involved in the action of plucking. Guitar picking is usually combined with Vibrato.

Exercise 89

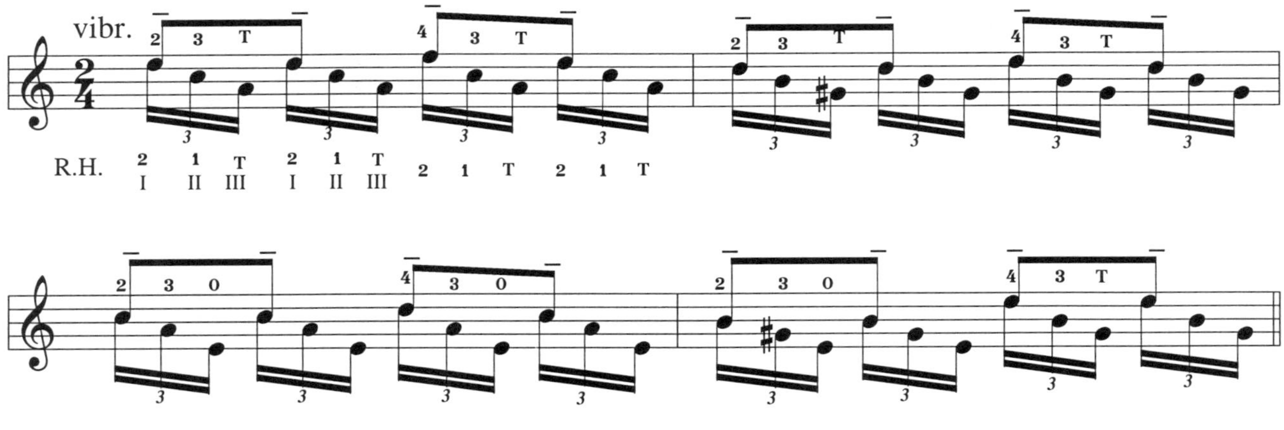


Exercise 90

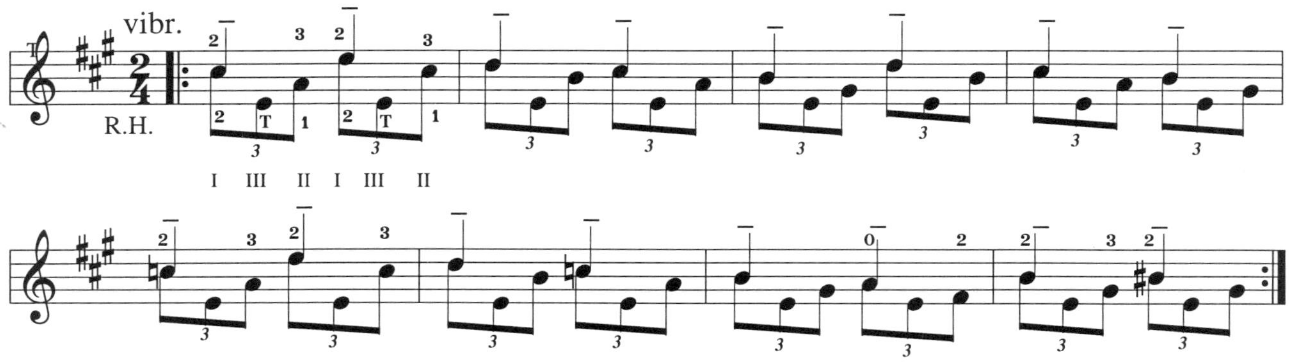


Exercise 91

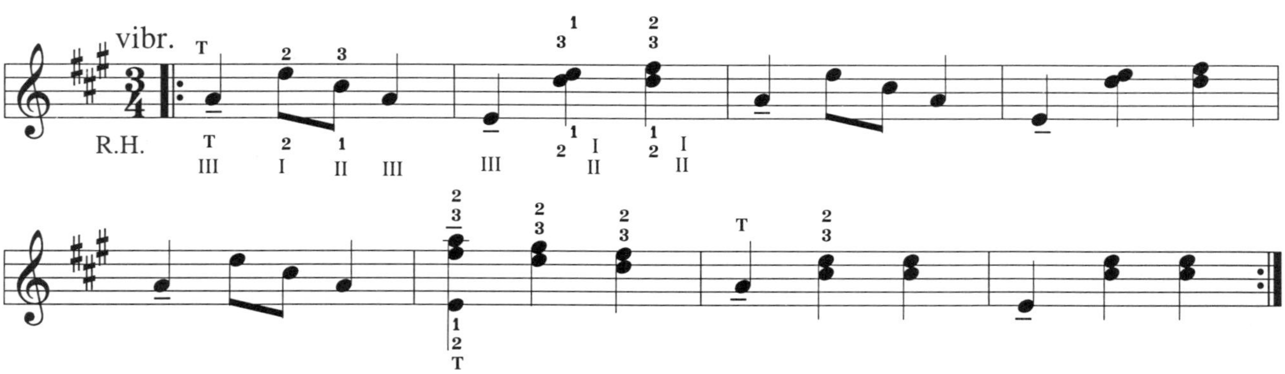

# Tricks and Special Effects

There are many little tricks that can be done with the balalaika: such as spins, twirls, and one-handed playing, as well as the drumming or knocking of the instrument for rhythmic effect (things which some Russian village lad would have used to show off in front of the girls a couple of centuries ago). Today these jolly devices are not only useful as theatrical effects, but also, along with the playing of Russian folk melodies, maintain the balalaika's direct link with its rustic origins.

## Squeak

A squeak can be produced by rubbing the ball of the hand sharply across the varnished front or side of the instrument. Best applied on the beat while playing left-hand pizzicato. When produced by several instruments at the same time gives the effect of a whistle.

*In this example the squeak is produced at the same moment that the left hand plucks the "A"-string. The right hand, having moved forward, is now in position to play the next note and the piece can continue uninterrupted.*

Exercise 92

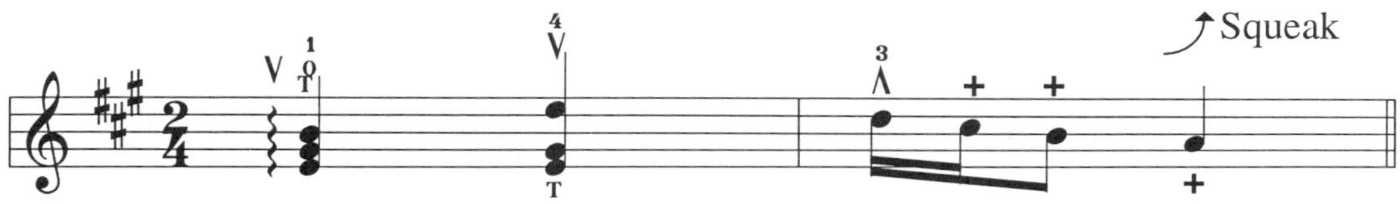


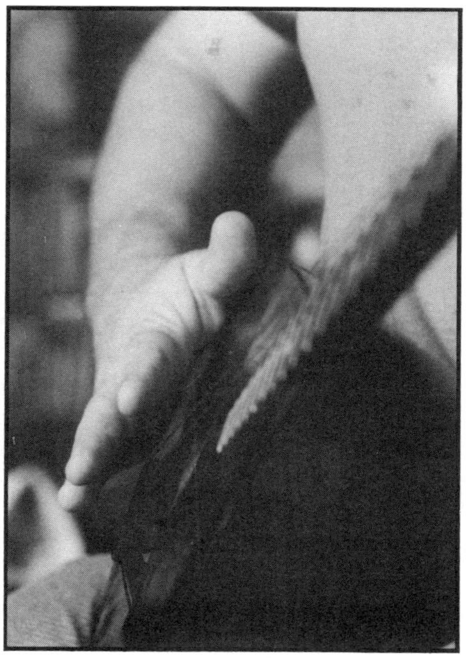

## Single Flip

The instrument is quickly flipped over 360 degrees by the left hand gently encircling the neck to hold it in the same plane, while the right hand either reaches down to the lower point of the balalaika's body and pulls it up and over in one deft movement or grasps it at the base of the strings and then spins it. The illustration shows the author's preferred method, with the little finger pushing one way and the remaining fingers the other.

(With practice double and triple saltos can also be achieved this way.)

Exercise 93

"Brightly Shines the Moon" – *Russian Folk Song*

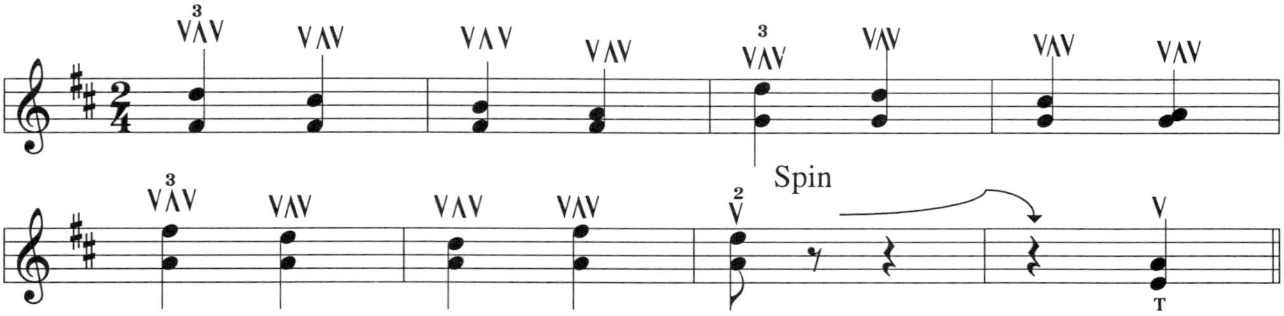

Finally, notes may be hammered or tapped and pulled off with one or other finger of the **right hand,** while the left hand holds a particular chord. In the example below, the top string is hammered from above by the flattened straight index finger, possibly backed up by the middle finger for extra dead weight. This finger then pulls off sideways (upwards), sounding the other two strings as it does so. If only single notes are to be sounded in this way they may be struck with the fingertip rather than the flattened finger.

Exercise 94

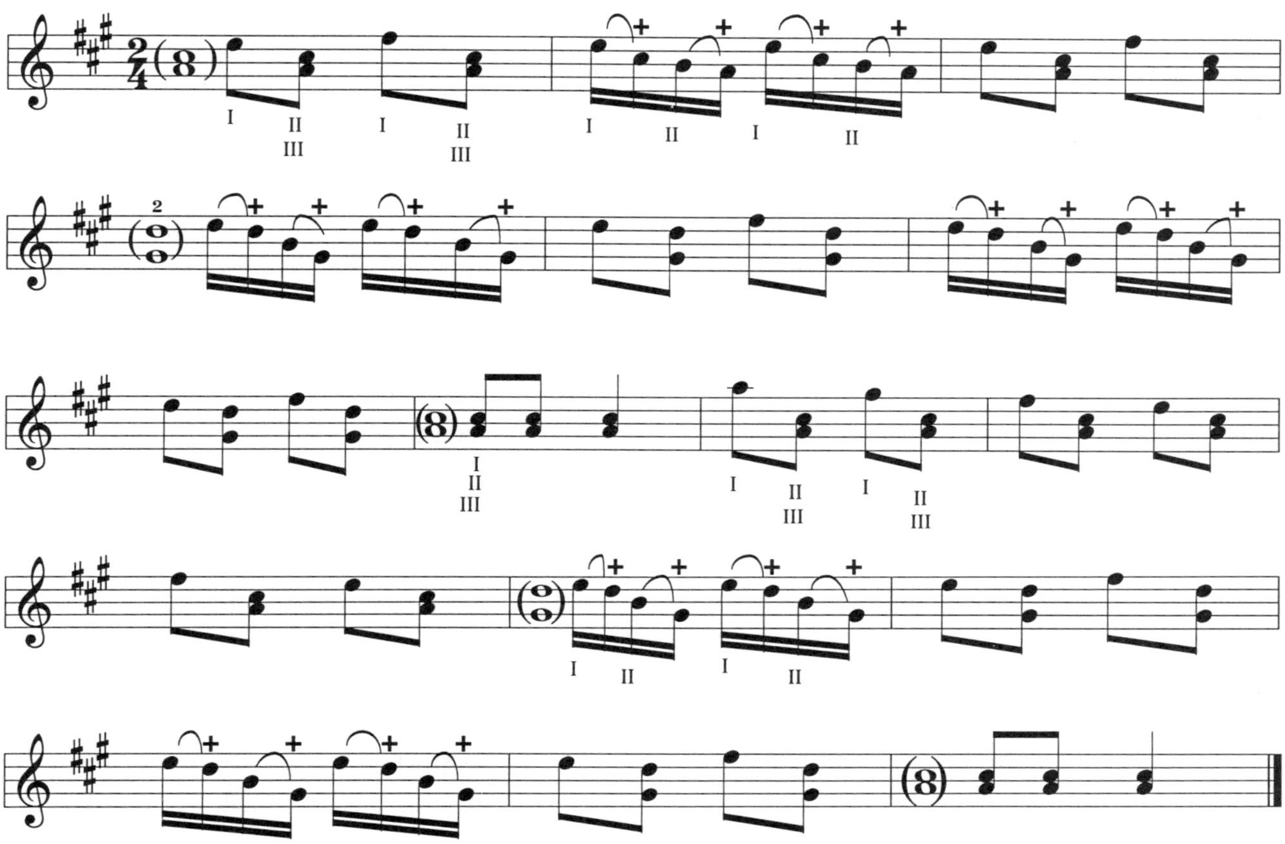

In the example, the chords shown in brackets are not played but just held by the left hand throughout subsequent bars until the next chord shown in brackets. Of each pair of notes the first is tapped or hammered (with the R.H.) and the second pulled off (with the R.H.).

**RHYTHMIC TAPPING** can be produced in a variety of ways in various places on the balalaika's body: either on the bridge, soundboard, base, or back to either imitate horses galloping, castanets playing, or even guns being fired.

**AN INTERESTING EFFECT** is produced by strumming out a rhythmic pattern with the index finger on strings deadened with the left hand. Such passages may be enclosed in brackets and be accompanied by an explanatory note, or the usual round note head may be replaced with an 'x' – the standard way of notating percussion.

**THE SECTION OF THE A-STRING** beyond the bridge may be plucked. The note that this will give tends to vary from instrument to instrument, but its occasional use can be combined with a flourish or circling movement of the right hand to great effect.

**IT IS POSSIBLE** to play whole melodies pizzicato with the left hand in a combination of pulling-off and hammering-on (occasionally the right hand may be used to "help out" by plucking the first note of a passage or a note too difficult to sound one-handed). While playing with one hand, the performance may be sensationalized in a number of ways: by flinging out the right arm and looking at it in amazement, lighting a cigarette with the free hand, combing one's hair, examining one's nails, standing up, walking about, supporting the outstretched instrument from below, and so on.
In repeated passages, one can either mime or actually play the first part and then put one's hand to one's ear to listen to the "echo" from the back of the hall for the repeat. If this is well executed, the audience will wonder at first where the sound is coming from: disbelief soon giving way to great amusement. These tricks may be executed with a high degree of dexterity, incorporating the plucking of notes alternately with the left or right hand while the balalaika is slowly spun or passed behind the back, under the legs, or over the head. It is apparently not unknown for the instrument to be flung up in the air as part of such a routine, although the instrument would need to be quite light and presumably not too valuable.

Exercise 95

# Some Extra Difficult Strokes

## Double Pizzicato

Sometimes difficult pizzicato passages occur similar to the following example.

In considering all the various possibilities it will be found that attempting to reverse the usual order of strokes and start the passage with an up-stroke would fail here (this would entail plucking the 3rd string upwards with the index finger – an impossibility).
The tempo is too fast for "guitar picking" to work effectively.
The usual solution of using double pizzicato on strings in the order I-I-III-I will cut short the notes on the top string which carry the melody and are supposed to ring.

No realistic alternative is available other than playing double pizzicato with strokes in the usual down/up order, starting with a down-stroke and conserving the natural emphasis on the first note of each bar. The middle string needs to be plucked upwards with the index finger while the thumb alternates between the 1st and 3rd strings.

Exercise 96

The index finger has to avoid inadvertently touching the top string while trying to 'hover' above the middle string awaiting its turn to play while the thumb has to skip clear over the middle string to alternately pluck the 1st and 3rd strings. Both fingers end up having to move, out of necessity breaking the hard and fast rules regarding finger and thumb being held stiffly and not moving during double pizzicato in order to achieve higher speeds. Here the index finger and thumb must simply learn to adjust to the unfamiliar angle and try to move no more than is necessary to achieve clean notes.
It is awkward but not impossible.

## Arpeggiato

Occasionally arpeggiato may be played downwards with the thumb and upwards with the flattened index finger to provide a series of even-sounding notes.

Exercise 97

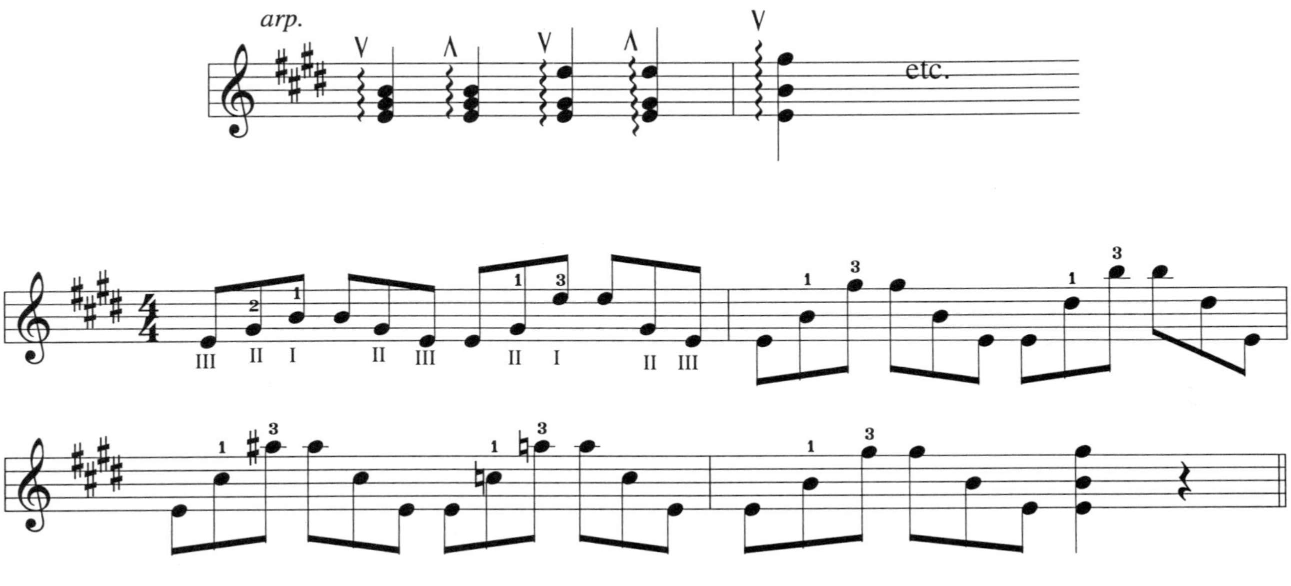

# General Advice on Practicing

Avoid sloppy, inaccurate playing. Repeating things wrong risks forming permanent bad habits. Pieces should be gone over slowly – if necessary even in slow motion – to make sure that every note is correct and sounds clearly.

Musicians often find that pieces need 'repairing' after a performance. When playing through a piece the player should find the weakest points in his or her playing and concentrate especially on these.

Practice the jumps between one left-hand position and another. This is particularly important for fast pizzicato passages, which it is good to practice using different rhythms, pairing notes together first one way, then another.

Exercise 98

from Polyanka - *Russian Folk Melody*

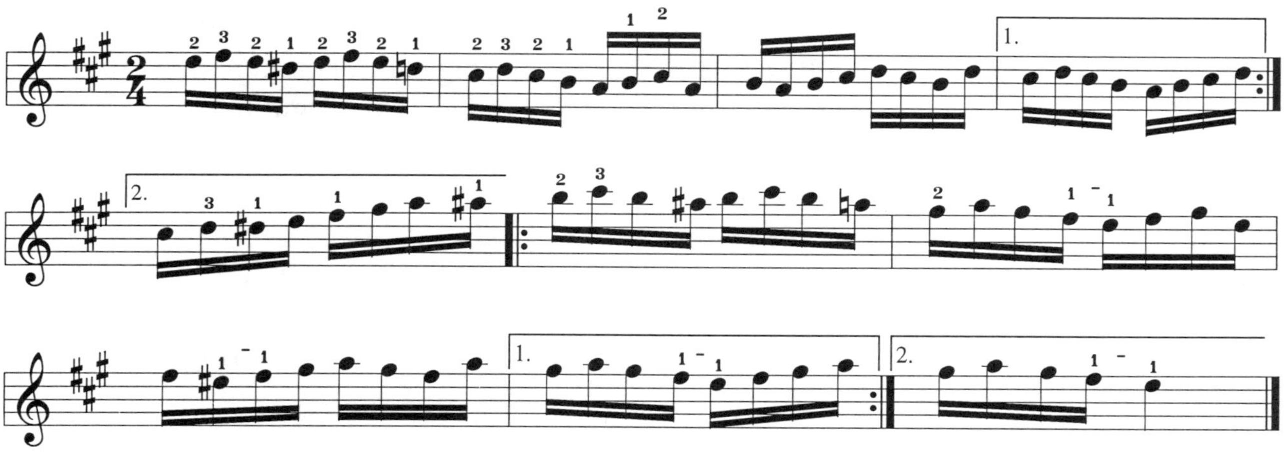

Exercise 99

Rhythm 1

Rhythm 2

At the same time ***relaxed playing is of paramount importance.*** Tension while playing tends to lead to tiring of the muscles and consequent loss of endurance, speed, and accuracy. As new playing techniques are learned, it is advisable to practice them, slowly at first, with attention being paid to *both* relaxation and accuracy. Although these two requirements may seem incompatible and hard to maintain at the same time, nevertheless if they are carefully observed the results will show later on in ease of playing complicated passages.

It is a good idea to practice loudly (maybe in front of a mirror), making both hands work harder than during ordinary playing. The skin needs to be sufficiently hard, otherwise the fingers are liable to get sore too quickly and force the player to cut short his or her practice time.

Regular careful practice is, of course, essential with all instruments. For the balalaika player daily practice is of additional importance for maintaining hard skin on the right-hand as well as left-hand fingers.

The beginner will find that at first the fingertips will hurt or blister. Gradually the skin on both hands will harden, allowing the player to play harder, louder, and longer. It is essential that this hardness of the skin is maintained. Not playing the instrument for some days will allow the fingertips to soften and during an eventual practice period (possibly extended to make up for lost time) the fingers are likely to blister, making playing painful or impossible for some time. This applies particularly to the 'playing' index finger of the right hand. Even small irregularities in the skin at the fingertip drastically affect the tone and can make playing very difficult. If necessary an emery board can be used to rub down and smooth the skin.

It is suggested that the student, when unable to practice out loud (or with full concentration) and short of time, daily maintain the fingers' hardness by deadening the strings with a cloth or blob of plasticine by the bridge and playing as hard as possible till the fingers hurt.

It is quite usual for one's playing to seem improved after a couple of days away from the instrument. The player should not be beguiled into complacency by this phenomenon which is akin to the motorist's car seeming to run better after a car wash or after the petrol tank has been filled.

Occasionally certain pieces, sometimes ones which the player has been playing quite happily for years, start to deteriorate. The fingers seem unable to cope with parts they knew so well and, worse still, no amount of practice seems to put them right.[1] The piece has been 'played out,' gone stale - *zaigralas'* (the Russians put it so well!). The only solution is to leave it for some months and then relearn it again from scratch.

**The following exercises** are recommended for daily practice. Close attention should be paid to the strength and clarity of each note. The strokes should all sound even, except where purposely accentuated. Fingers, having pressed a note, should remain in position until they

---

[1] It is hard to explain this peculiar phenomenon, but it is one with which all professional musicians will be familiar.

*need* to be removed, and then are lifted off vertically. Before playing, each finger should, ideally, already be in position above the string and should fall strongly and vertically down onto the fingerboard.

For developing even down and up pizzicato strokes the player is recommended to play the appropriate exercises through, starting the first note with a down-stroke; then through again, starting with an up-stroke. Try to make the exercise sound the same whichever means is used. Try using different rhythmic patterns and accents.

The tempo of the exercises should be increased or lessened according to the ability of the pupil. Repeat the exercises that cause the greatest difficulty.

# DAILY EXERCISES

*for strumming:*

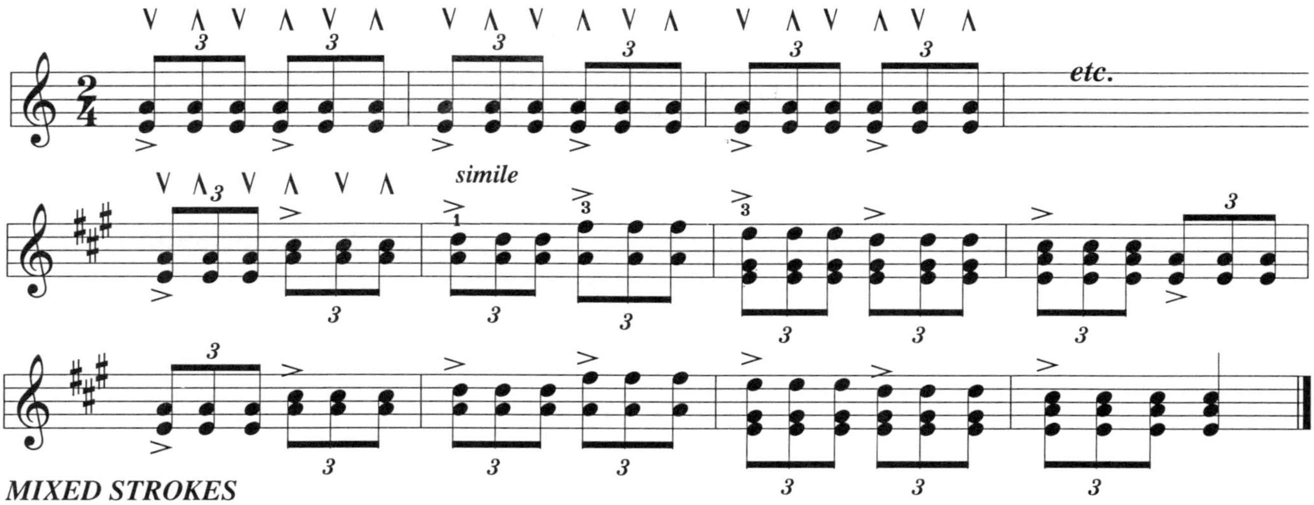


*MIXED STROKES*

*strumming/tremolo*

*large rolls/strumming/tremolo*

*upward rolls/strumming/tremolo*

*large & small rolls/tremolo*

*double or single pizzicato*

*mixed single and double pizzicato*

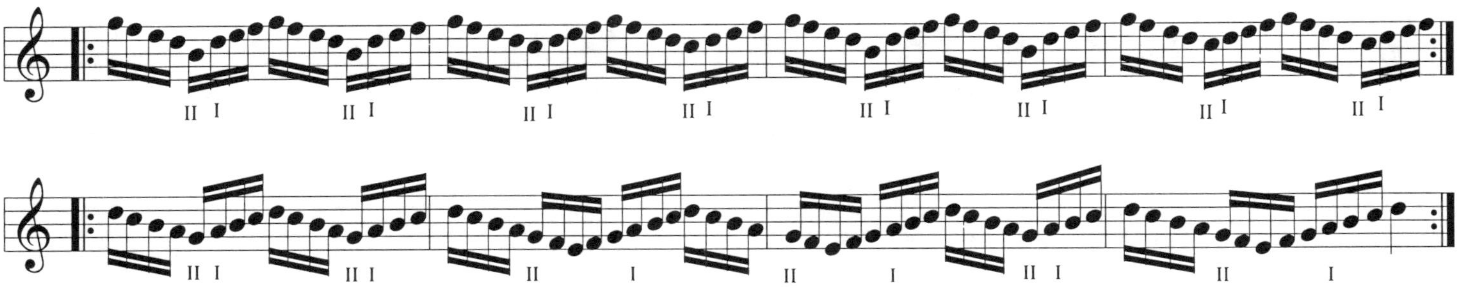

**Four exercises for developing fast, accurate pizzicato.**

Based by the author on a favorite exercise of Mikhail Rozhkov – a balalaika virtuoso renowned for the unsurpassed speed and clarity of his pizzicato playing.

*Play through using each of the alternative fingerings.*

*Experiment with accentuating different notes in the pattern.*

①

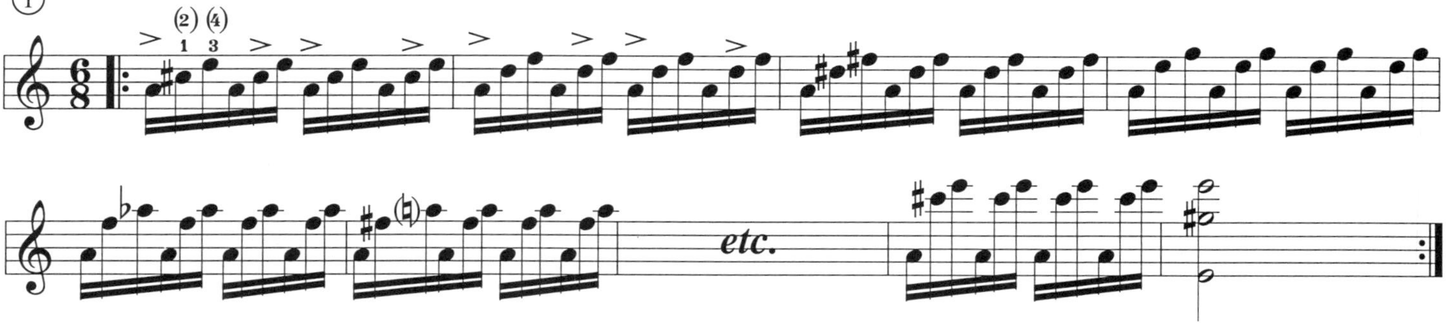


②

③

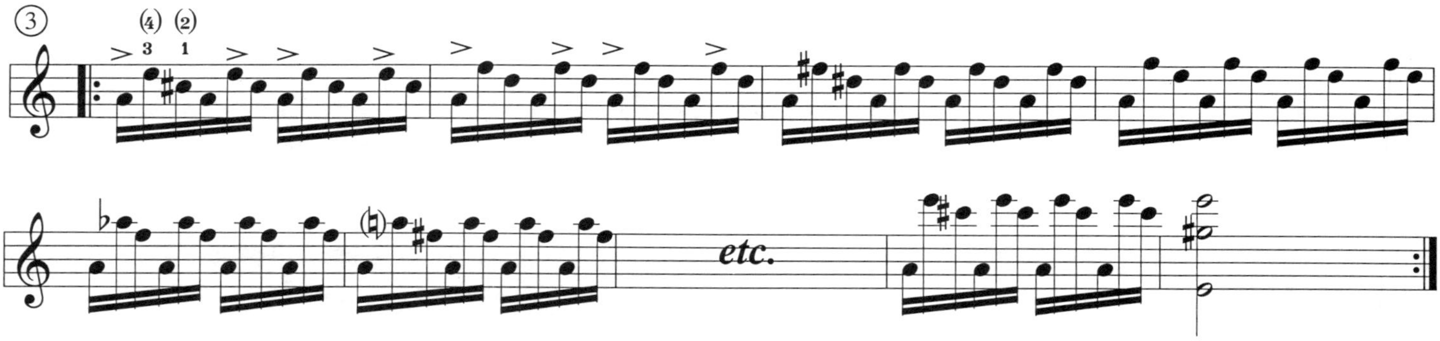


④

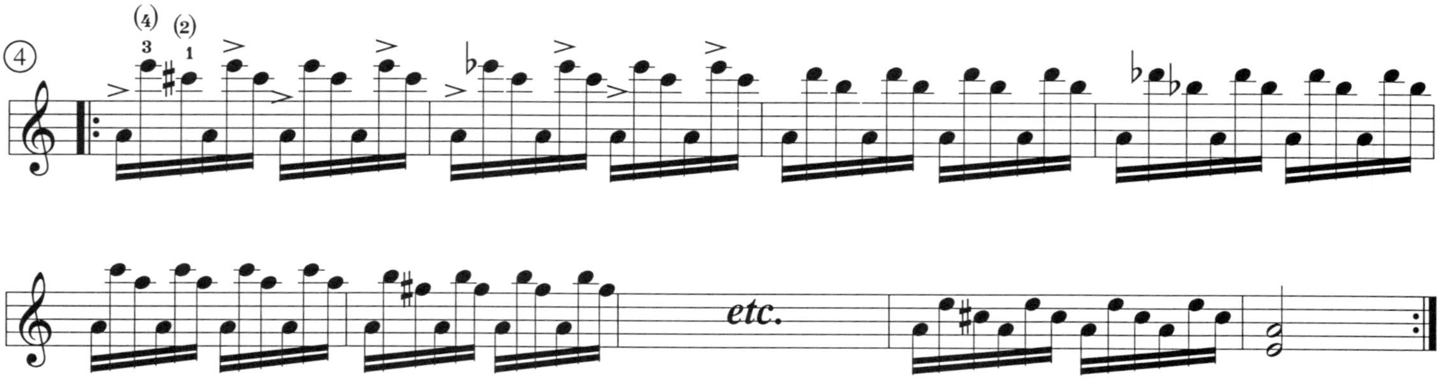

The following Schradek violin exercises have been put to excellent use by players of a variety of stringed instruments, including the balalaika and domra. Practice them using both single and double pizzicato, at a speed within your ability. Make sure each note sounds clearly and evenly. Try to keep the hands as relaxed as possible, exerting no more effort than is needed to achieve the required clarity and volume. Pay close attention to the left hand, making sure the fingers fall strongly and are raised with elasticity. Repeat the exercises that cause the greatest difficulty.

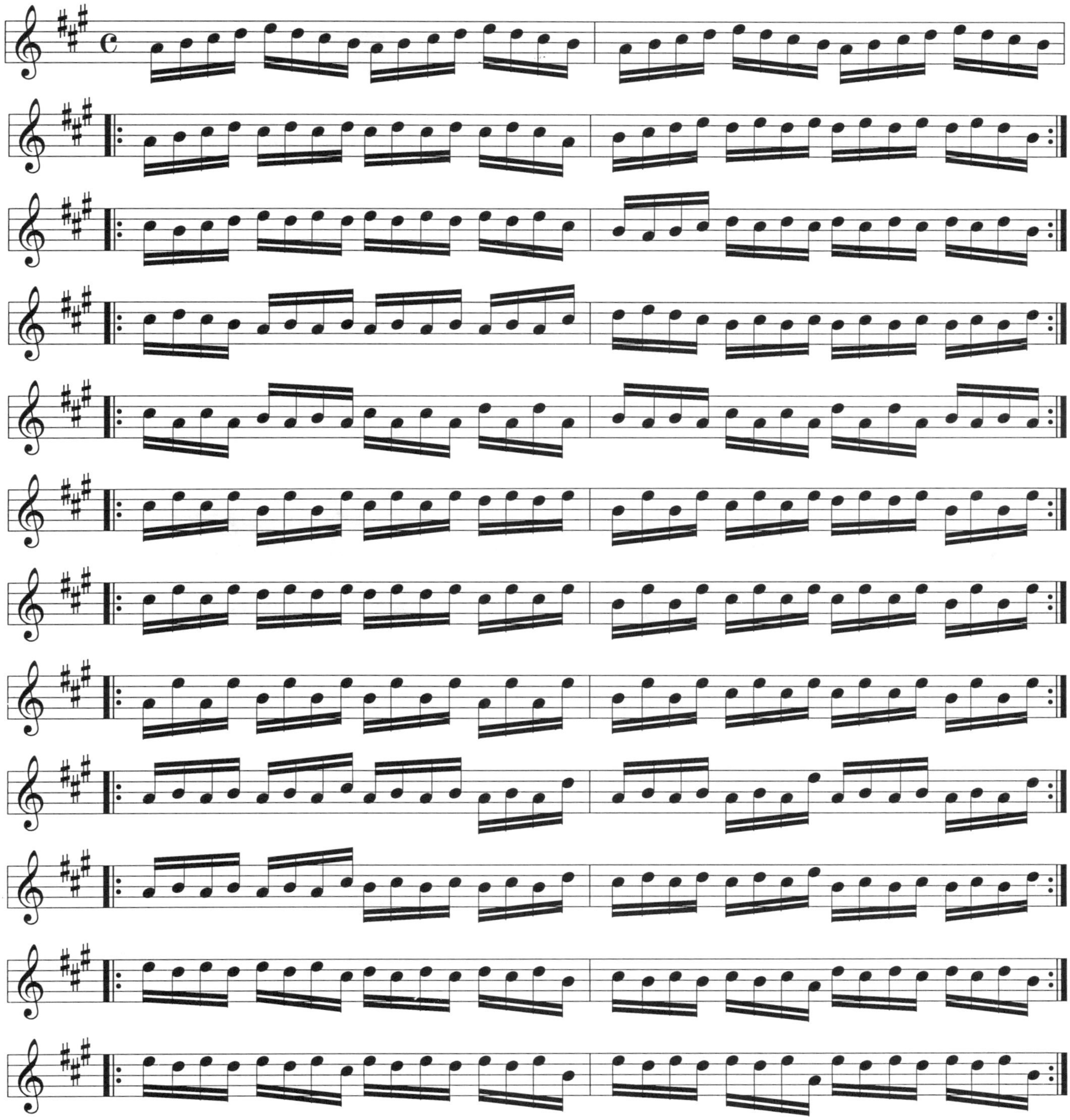

1.
2.
3.
4.
5.
6.
7.
8.
9.
10.
11.
12.

13.

14.

15.

16.

17.

18.

19.

20.

21.

22.

23.

24.

25.

# Glossary of Musical Signs

| | | |
|---|---|---|
| > | accent | appears above the note |
| ♯ | sharp | placed before the note raises it a semitone (one fret) |
| ♭ | flat | placed before the note lowers it a semitone (one fret) |
| ♮ | natural | cancels out a preceding sharp or flat |
| x | double sharp | raises the note by two semitones (two frets) |
| ♭♭ | double flat | lowers the note by two semitones (two frets) |
| ***ff*** | fortissimo | very loud |
| ***f*** | forte | loud |
| ***mf*** | mezzo forte | medium loud |
| ***mp*** | mezzo piano | medium soft |
| ***p*** | piano | soft |
| ***pp*** | pianissimo | very soft |
| *Fine* | The End | used to show the end of the piece |
| *pizz.* | pizzicato | plucking |
| *D.C.* | Da Capo | repeat from the beginning |
| *D.S.* | Dal Segno | repeat from the sign |
| *Rit.* | Ritardando | slowing down |
|  | cresc. or crescendo | getting louder |
| 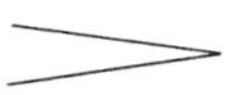 | dim. or diminuendo | getting softer |
|  | gliss. or glissando | sliding (see appropriate section) |

 before a chord: arpeggiato or a small roll

 before a chord: a large roll

**T** is used in this tutor to indicate the thumb. (In Russian music: б or Б, б.п., ⊔ or ⊓.)

\+ above or below a note indicates it is plucked or hammered with the left hand

 A dot above or below a note means the note is played staccato, i.e. sounds very briefly.

 A line above a note (or below if the stem is upwards), indicates it is emphasized slightly and held to its full time value.

 A small circle above a note indicates a natural harmonic.

 A diamond above an ordinary note indicates a false harmonic. The diamond indicates the fret at which the harmonic is produced - the ordinary note below indicates the base note being held.

 fermata — hold note or rest longer than written value

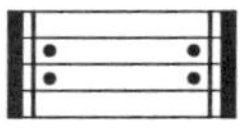 repeat signs — the section between the signs is repeated

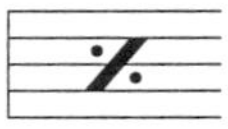 same as the preceding bar or bars

 A ligature indicates legato, smooth, connected notes without breaks; often indicates tremolo.

 One or two slanted lines through the note stem indicate strumming.

 Three short slanted lines through the note stem indicate tremolo.

VΛ Above a note indicates a down- and up-stroke, respectively. (Sometimes: ⊓ V is used.)

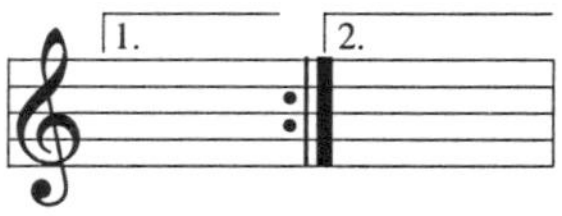

Used with repeated sections to indicate parts to be played only the first and second times, respectively.

 slur — When joining two different notes this indicates that the notes are run together. The first note is made to sound for its full duration, the second note more briefly. Very often the second note is played with left-hand pizzicato, especially in descending passages.

 tie — When joining two notes of the same pitch, this indicates that the first note is held on for the duration of the second note without a break.

| NOTE: | | WRITTEN: | REST: | NO. OF BEATS |
|---|---|---|---|---|
| Whole | (semi-breve) | 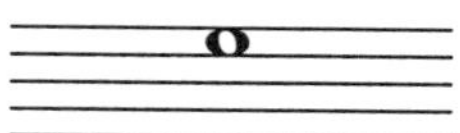 | 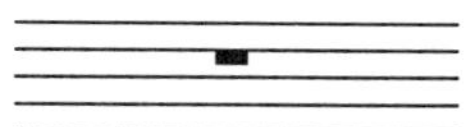 | 4 |
| Half | (minim) | 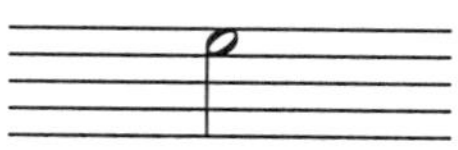 | 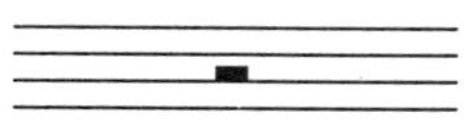 | 2 |
| Quarter | (crotchet) |  |  | 1 |
| Eighth | (quaver) |  | 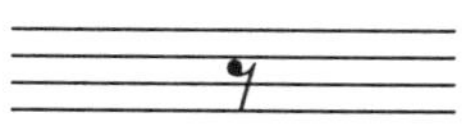 | 1/2 |
| Sixteenth | (semi-quaver) |  | 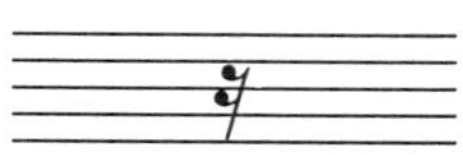 | 1/4 |
| A dot after the note adds 50% value to the note. | | | | |

# Russian Musical Terms

The tempo and manner of playing in balalaika music is often indicated in Russian rather than in Italian. The most commonly used Russian terms are listed below.

| | |
|---|---|
| более, больше | more |
| бряцание | strumming |
| быстрее | faster |
| быстро | fast |
| вариация | variation |
| вибрато | vibrato |
| в начальном /прежнем темпе | at the initial /former speed |
| возбужденно | agitatedly |
| в темпе | in time |
| в темпе марша | tempo of a march |
| вальса | waltz |
| полонеза | polonaise |
| мазурки | mazurka |
| польки | polka |
| выразительно | expressively |
| гитара | guitar |
| грациозно | graciously |
| громко | loudly |
| громче | louder |
| довольно | quite |
| долго | long |
| еще | again, more |
| еще раз | once again |
| живо, живее | lively, livelier |
| задерживая | holding back |
| задушевно | soulfully |
| замедляя | slowing |
| замирая | dying away |
| затухая | extinguishing |
| и | and |
| игриво | playfully |
| каденция | cadence |
| как | as, like |
| легко | lightly |
| марш | march |
| медленно, медленнее | slowly, slower |
| мягко | softly |
| на | on, at |
| напевно | song-like |
| начальный | initial, beginning |
| не | not, no |
| нежно | affectionately |
| немного | a little |
| неторопливо | unhurriedly |
| оживленно | lively |
| отчетливый | definitely |
| очень | very |
| пауза | pause |
| певуче | singing |
| первый | first |
| повторить | repeat |
| подвижно | not too fast |
| постепенно | gradually |
| с | with, from |
| свободно | freely |
| с выражением | with expression |
| с движением | with movement |
| сдержанно | restrainedly |
| скоро | quickly |
| слишком | too |
| спеша | hurriedly |
| спокойно | calmly |
| струна | string |
| так | thus |
| тема | theme |
| темп | tempo |
| тихо, тише | quietly, quieter |
| торопясь | hurriedly |
| тот же | the same |
| тремоло | tremolo |
| умеренно | moderately |
| ускоряя | speeding up |
| ф-но, фортепиано | piano |
| чуть | a little |
| широко | broadly, expansively |
| штрих | stroke |
| шутливо | playfully |
| Др. | roll |
| обр. др. | upward roll |
| б (ог Б) | thumb |
| Б. П. | thumb |
| У. П. | index finger |
| обработка | arrangement |
| переложение | transposition |
| редакция | edited by |
| арп. | arpeggiato |

# Short Introduction to Timing

| No. of beats *(Count to oneself...)* | 1 *"one - and..."* | | 2 *"two - and..."* | | 3 *"three - and..."* | | 4 *"four - and..."* | |
|---|---|---|---|---|---|---|---|---|
| Whole note (semi-breve) | 𝅝 | | | | | | | |
| Half note (minim) | 𝅗𝅥 | | | | 𝅗𝅥 | | | |
| Quarter note (crotchet) | ♩ | | ♩ | | ♩ | | ♩ | |
| Eighth note (quaver) | ♪ | ♪ | ♪ | ♪ | ♪ | ♪ | ♪ | ♪ |
| Sixteenth note (semi-quaver) | 𝅘𝅥𝅯𝅘𝅥𝅯 | 𝅘𝅥𝅯𝅘𝅥𝅯 | 𝅘𝅥𝅯𝅘𝅥𝅯 | 𝅘𝅥𝅯𝅘𝅥𝅯 | 𝅘𝅥𝅯𝅘𝅥𝅯 | 𝅘𝅥𝅯𝅘𝅥𝅯 | 𝅘𝅥𝅯𝅘𝅥𝅯 | 𝅘𝅥𝅯𝅘𝅥𝅯 |

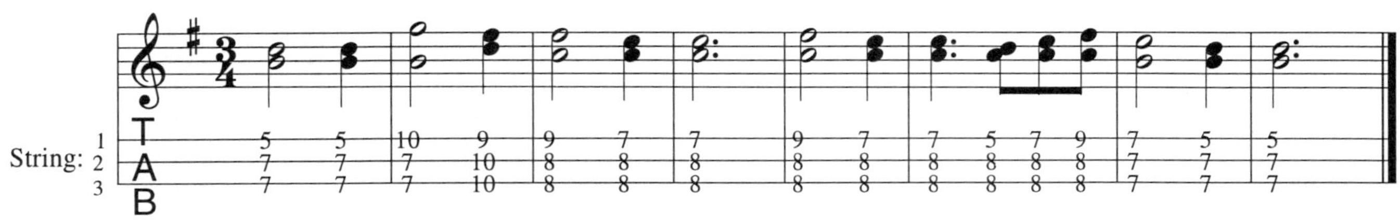


The normal system for written music uses five lines and begins with the treble clef sign:  (or  for bass instruments). Sharps and flats follow, then the Time Signature (see the above example).

The cipher system tablature for the balalaika uses three lines representing strings 1, 2, and 3. The numbers represent the fret being pressed.

Vertical lines divide up the passage into equal sections called bars, each of which has the same number of beats indicated by the Time Signature.

The lower number in a Time Signature indicates the value or duration of each whole beat, while the upper number shows the number of those beats in each bar.

For clarity, tails of notes may point up or down and the "flags" of notes of the same beat joined together (♫ instead of ♪♪).

The first note of each bar is usually stressed slightly.

It helps greatly to count the beats as "one-and-two-and..." to oneself while playing. For passages involving sixteenth notes (semi-quavers), it is practical to divide the count up still further.

*See also section on Rests in Glossary.*

# A Brief History Of The Balalaika

# A Brief History of the Balalaika

Exactly when the balalaika first appeared isn't known. What *is* certain, however, is that the instrument is native to Russia and probably stemmed from another, earlier Russian folk instrument – the domra. The round-bodied, two-stringed domra, reputedly the favorite instrument of the "skomorokhi" (the wandering minstrels in the Middle Ages) is believed to have been first brought to Russia from across the steppes in the 13th Century Tartar invasion.

The earliest known reference to the balalaika is to be found in a document dated 1688 - an official report on the punishing of two men caught playing the instrument in flagrant defiance of the 1648 edict of Czar Alexei Mikhailovich, which banned the playing of all 'devilish' musical instruments. All instruments were to be confiscated and burned, and transgressors faced a public flogging and banishment to outlying regions of Russia (which is, in fact, where folk instrumental art eventually survived, far from official control).

Back then, the instrument had a semi-spherical, oval, or triangular body and a long neck with 5 - 7 movable tied gut frets. Almost all instruments were home-made and their shape, number of strings and tuning tended to vary. However, two or three strings and a triangular body with a back made of four triangular wooden slats seems to have been most common. Balalaikas were played in rural communities, enjoying wide popularity until being superceded by foreign newcomers: first the accordion and then the 7-string guitar in the 19th Century.

The balalaika had all but fallen into oblivion when it was "rediscovered" by a nobleman and amateur violinist, Vasili Vasilievich Andreyev, who chanced to hear the playing of a peasant (a certain Antip) on his family estate. Andreyev was eventually to be responsible for re-popularizing the instrument, helping it gain respectability and placing it permanently on the concert platform. This tireless champion not only learned to play the balalaika well, but also initiated a number of changes and improvements to the instrument. Apart from permanent chromatically-arranged metal frets and changes in design to improve its acoustic qualities, he had different sizes made, so that when the balalaika reemerged, it was not only as a solo instrument, but as an orchestral one too – gaining immediate popularity for collective playing.

Andreyev's first solo public performance in 1886 in St. Petersburg caused a sensation. Soon afterwards he formed a small circle of balalaika enthusiasts, playing the full range of newly improved instruments. Their first public performance was in March 1888. Soon this group was expanded to form a larger ensemble called the Great Russian Imperial Balalaika Orchestra, incorporating the domra and gusli, which by then Andreyev had also redesigned and improved. He also composed several pieces for the balalaika.

Of the luthiers Andreyev commissioned to make his redesigned models: Ivanov, Pasyerbsky, and Nalimov, it was with the latter that he formed the most permanent and productive relationship. Nalimov made and repaired instruments in the workshop on Andreyev's estate, producing instruments which were later emulated by all the best makers. At one stage, while money was short, Nalimov and Andreyev removed all the doors and window-sills at

Andreyev's ancestral home, having discovered them to be made of pure mountain maple – ideal for the bodies of balalaikas and domras. Today Nalimov's prima balalaikas are regarded, along with those by Sotsky, much as Stradivari among violins, with Pasyerbsky, Galinis, Snegiryov and later Tokarev, D. Rodin, Yemelyanov and others following. Among contemporary makers, Mikhailov, Zaitsev, Pavlov, Necheporenko and, in particular, Andreas Gerth in Berlin deserve mention.

The acclaim and popularity with which Andreyev's orchestra was greeted in Russia was soon to be echoed abroad when, in 1909, the orchestra embarked on a series of world tours. The stir these concerts caused led to the appearance of balalaika orchestras all over the world and, consequently, a great demand for both instruments and music. (According to Russian statistics, Britain in the 1920's was second only to Russia in its number of active balalaika orchestras.)

Although changing musical tastes and fashions led to a temporary decline in the balalaika's fortunes in many Western countries since those early years, today there is a noticeable resurgence of interest in the instrument both in Europe and in particular in the United States, where dozens of amateur orchestras are to be found. In the Soviet Union the instrument has consistently held its place of special reverence; countless amateur and professional orchestras are to be heard in every part of the country performing a wide variety of folk and classical pieces. Playing standards, as well as literature for the instrument, continue to improve and expand along with the number of young virtuosi the conservatoires turn out each year. Among pieces specially written for the solo balalaika are several suites and concerti with folk or symphony orchestra accompaniment.

Vasili Vasilievich Andreyev (born 15th January 1861 in the town of Bezhetsk) died on the night of 25th December 1918, having caught a chill during a concert tour. In 1905 the Tzar awarded Andreyev special funding plus a salary for life in recognition of his services to the Russian nation, during the course of which he had used up his entire fortune. Coming under the sponsorship of the Czar, the orchestra was renamed the Imperial Russian Orchestra.

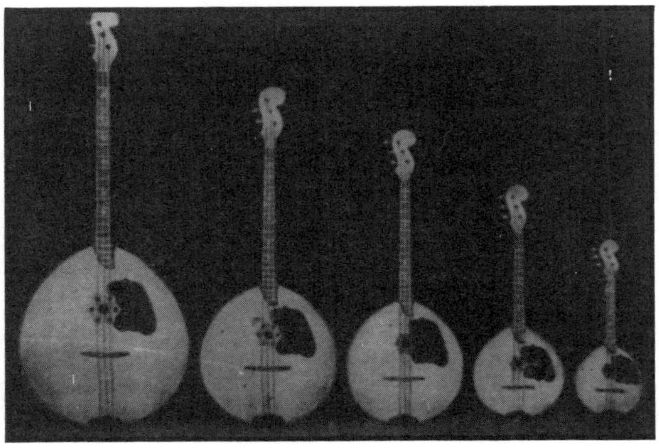

**Complete set of DOMRAS**
←
Bass, Tenor, Alto, Prima & Piccolo

**Complete set of BALALAIKAS**
→
Contrabass, Bass, Alto, Secundo, & Prima

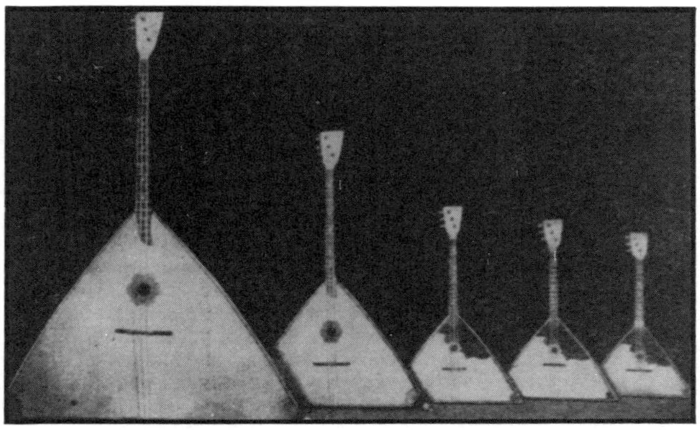

Several of the different sizes of balalaika and domra created experimentally by Andreyev subsequently fell into disuse as in time their role in the orchestra was found to be superfluous. Among these were the descant, piccolo and tenor balalaikas, whose disappearance coincided with the appearance of the piccolo domra and secundo balalaika, and also with a change from the original to present-day tunings. The three-string contrabass domra (originally tuned ADG) is rarely used, although the four-string variety[1] is quite common, especially in all-domra ensembles.

---

[1] The four-string domra was reconstructed by G.P. Lyubimov together with luthier S.F. Burov in 1908. Tuned in fifths, with the exception of the contrabass (which is in fourths), the four string domra is preferred in Southern Russia and the Ukraine. From Muscovy to Petersburg the 3-string domra prevails. Three- and four-string domras are rarely to be found together in the same orchestra.

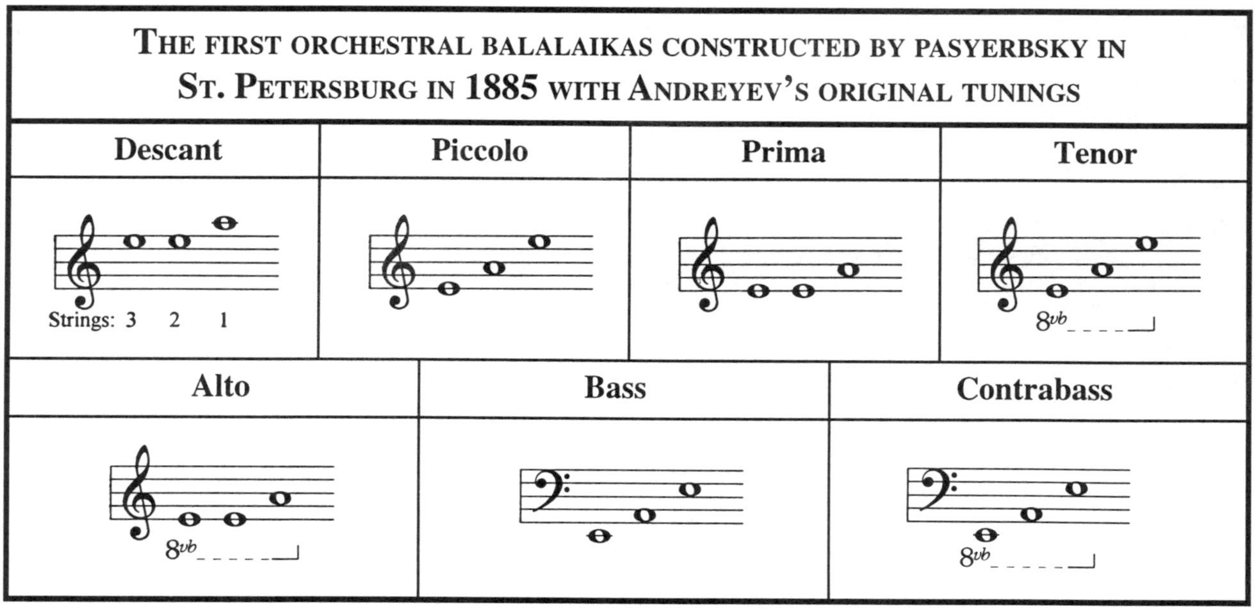


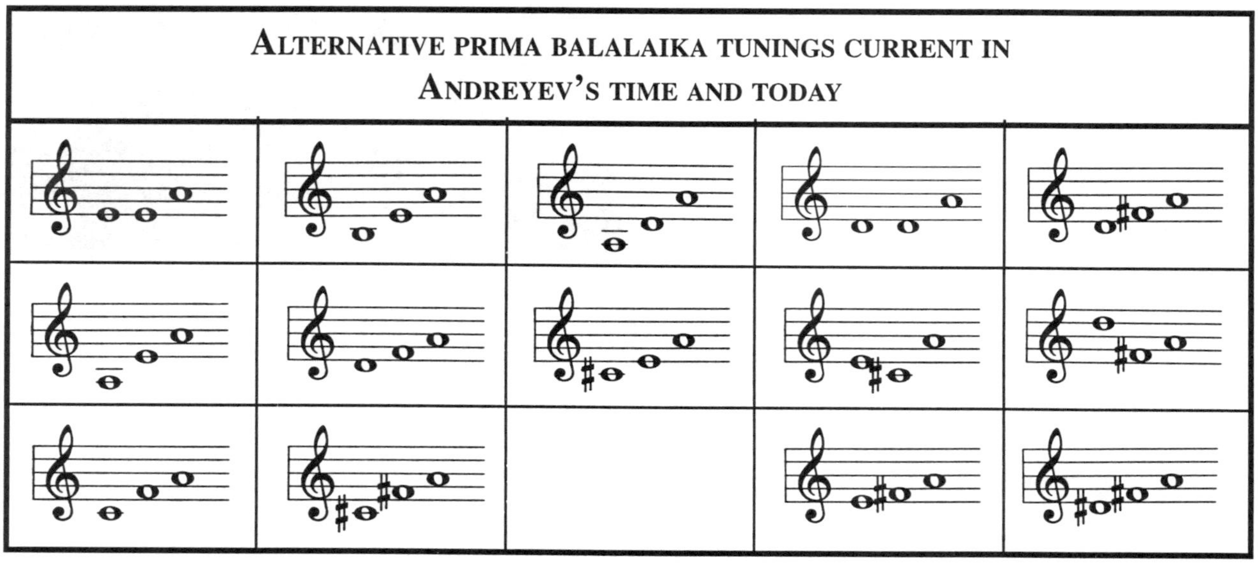


The first one is the tuning adopted by Andreyev as being most suitable for solo and orchestral playing. It allows the instrument to carry the melody while all three strings are being played.

The other tunings are less versatile, and better suited for strumming chords to accompany singing. Although rarely encountered, they are still occasionally to be found in use in some rural areas, with particular tunings being subject to regional preference.[1]

---

[1] See: V.K. Galakhov (of Orel Conservatoire): "Various Tunings of the Folk Balalaika" printed as part of the collection *Studies in Musical Folklore (Izuchenie muzykalnogo folklora)* Rostov-on-Don, 1986.

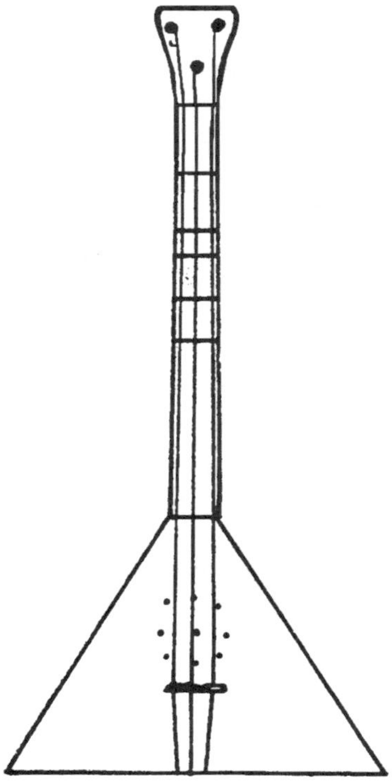

**Primitive Balalaika**

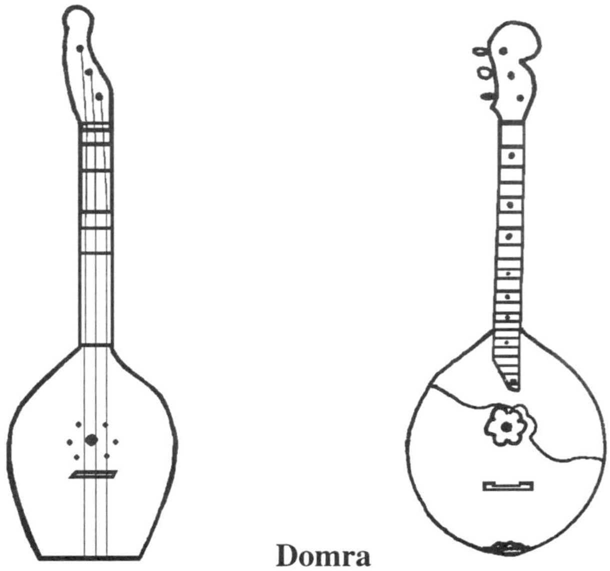

**Domra**

As it was - and as it is today

A 19th-century advertisement for the newly improved chromatic balalaikas. Instruments of various quality ranged in price from 5 - 200 roubles.

Andreyev's Circle of Balalaika Enthusiasts with Pasyerbsky instruments (1880's). The players were all professional people (doctors, lawyers, etc.), and included Nasonov, Privalov and Fomin, each of whom in his own way did much to further the balalaika's cause.

Andreyev's Imperial Russian Orchestra (circa 1900). In the foreground the recently reconstructed domras (left) and gusli (right).

The Moscow-based Osipov Folk Orchestra. Such present-day orchestras, in addition to the full range of balalaikas and domras, usually use table-size gusli (center) as well as bayans (button accordions) and folk or symphony woodwind instruments. Some orchestras consist of stringed instruments only.

Some balalaikas are inlaid with wood or mother-of-pearl designs. In the photograph – one of the author's home-made balalaikas.

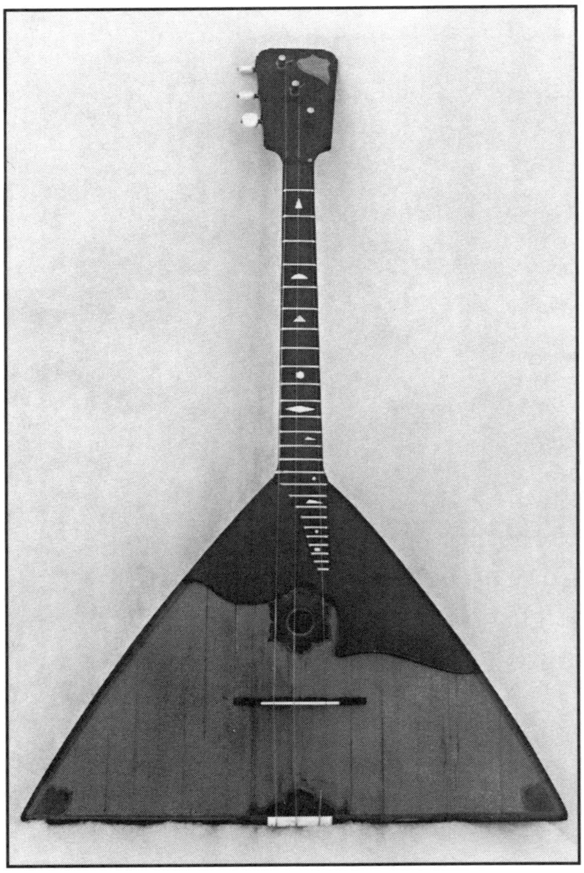

Prima Balalaika by S. I. Nalimov. No: 168 dated 1914 - one of the last produced.
The label inside reads:

No.____________
Made by S. I. Nalimov
under the direction of V. V. Andreyev
in the village of Mar'ino-Andreyevskoye
Year___________

Semeon Ivanovich Nalimov worked directly under Vassili Andreyev's supervision in the latter's own workshop. His instruments are noted for their accurate workmanship and pure sound. They are also known to be more 'moody' than many other instruments – sounding better under certain weather conditions and when played consistently.
A total of at least 170 balalaikas (mostly primas) were made, and 131 domras. They were all numbered along with the year. **(See "Balalaika Master Luthier" (Balalaechnikh del master) by Anatolii Peresada of Krasnodar for listing of known instruments and present (1982) owners.)*
Nalimov's work clearly shows the evolvement of the instrument as Andreyev experimented and initiated improvements.
Early Nalimov balalaikas had a limited number of frets, a traditional little house window soundhole, flush veneer scratchplate; later models had 24 frets, 'petal' shaped round soundhole, ebony veneer scratchplate glued onto the soundboard and finally, in later models, a raised, overhanging scratchplate.
Most 'Nalimov's' were plain, although a few were encrusted with mother-of-pearl.
The celebrated artist Bilibin – famous for his Russian Fairy Tale illustrations – was a friend of Andreyev's and helped redesign the balalaika in an attractive traditional Russian style.
Most Nalimov prima balalaikas today have been re-made (like the author's balalaika above), having an overhanging scratchplate added, a new fingerboard and extra frets for increased range. Many have lost some of their volume in the improvement process. Others suffered similarly from bad repairs, or from having their soundboard rubbed down after splits were fixed. Despite this, the sweetness and purity of tone of Nalimov's instruments is highly prized among balalaika players.

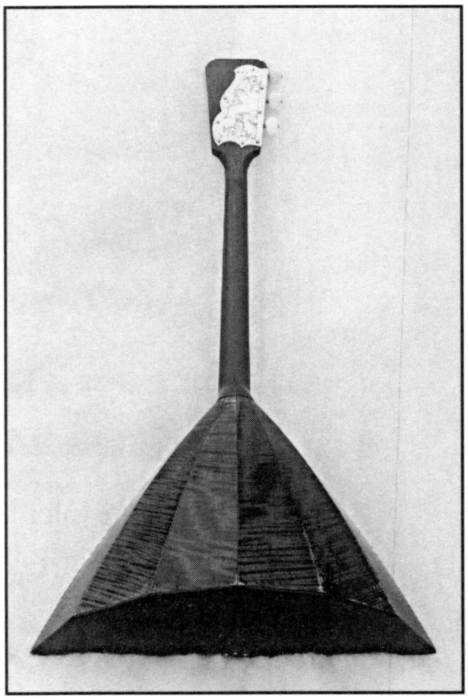

Dark-stained maple back, rosewood neck and head. Like other balalaika makers Nalimov occasionally used rosewood instead of maple. Sometimes the back-ribs had jutting-out veins between sections. While most of his successful contemporaries (Pasyerbsky, Ziuzin, Ogloblin) preferred seven-piece backs, Nalimov's primas were exclusively six-piece. Later generations of luthiers would follow Nalimov's design. Few, if any, seven-piece back primas are made today, with the notable exception of those outstanding instruments by the recently deceased Moscow engineer-turned-balalaika-maker Kupfer.

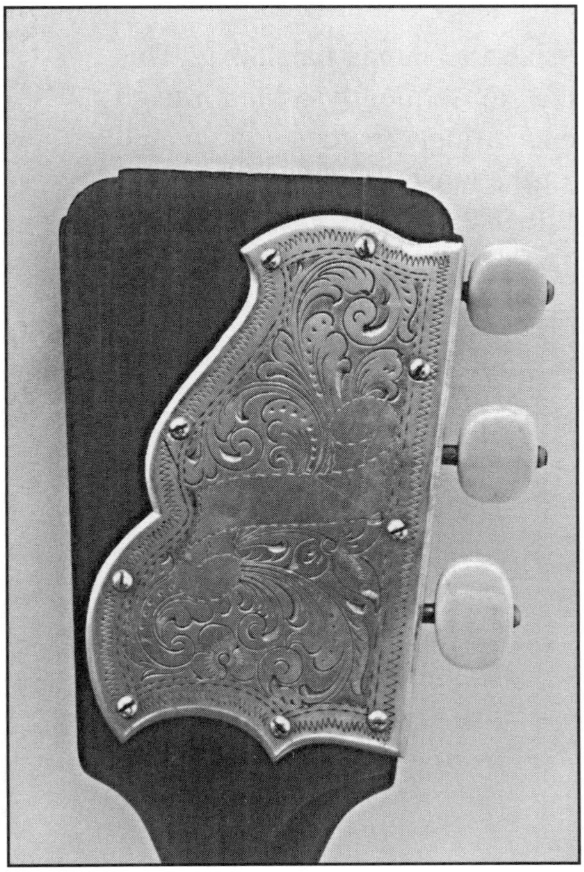

Instruments made before the 1917 Bolshevik revolution were noted for their high level of craftsmanship. The Nalimov has ivory tuning peg buttons with engraved silver machine-head back cover.
Nowadays even the better Soviet instruments have notoriously inaccurate and unreliable machine-heads with a plain, utilitarian brass, steel or brushed aluminium cover.

Few Nalimov instruments have survived without needing repairs to cracks in the soundboard. An unusual feature common to all Nalimovs is the dot marking the bridge position on the soundboard.

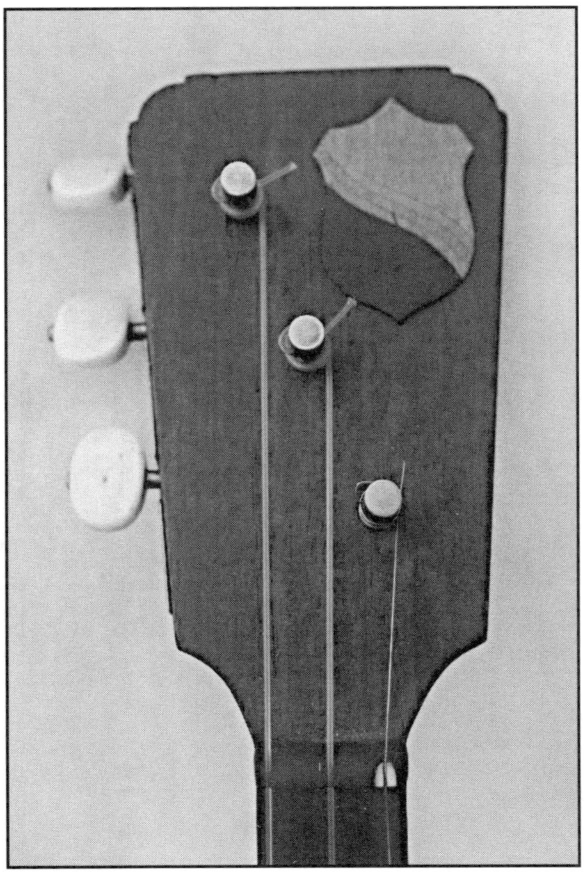

Nalimov's balalaikas were invariably decorated with a two-tone shield with a diagonal tricolor strip – as here. The colors were meant to represent the White, Blue and Red of the Czarist flag.
Nalimov domras were decorated with a similar badge, but slightly different in outline.

Ziuzin (St. Petersburg) secunda balalaika. This instrument has a subsequently-added raised scratchplate extended fingerboard.

Ziuzin was one of the most prolific producers of balalaikas at the turn of the century, making mostly cheap, but also a few acoustically better, more expensive models. In order to encoürage balalaika production, Andreyev gave complimentary samples of Nalimov instruments to the leading luthiers of his day, for them to emulate. Some makers, (Ziuzin and Galinis among them) copied the Nalimov tricolor insignia for the heads of some of their instruments.

Playable miniature balalaika made by Milton Cherin (New York) 1980.

Sometimes plastic sleeves are threaded over the strings beyond the bridge. This is to facilitate the playing of vibrato and also to prevent any renegade sharp ends from snagging the player's trousers. It can also deaden any unwanted out-of-tune ringing from that section of the strings beyond the bridge, a problem with certain instruments. (Some players prefer that this part of the A-string not only remain uncovered, but also be tuned to a particular note which can be then plucked during playing or as part of a 'trick.')

Prima by Sotsky, Moscow 1939. Modern in design, tending to be less in need of reconstruction than Nalimovs, Sotsky's instruments are consistently loud and have excellent tone.

Very little information is available about the maker himself. His orchestral sizes of balalaika and domra are almost always outstanding too. Many of his instruments come decorated with a Nalimov-style tricolor heart on the headpiece. Rosewood back, ebony neck, ivory buttons.

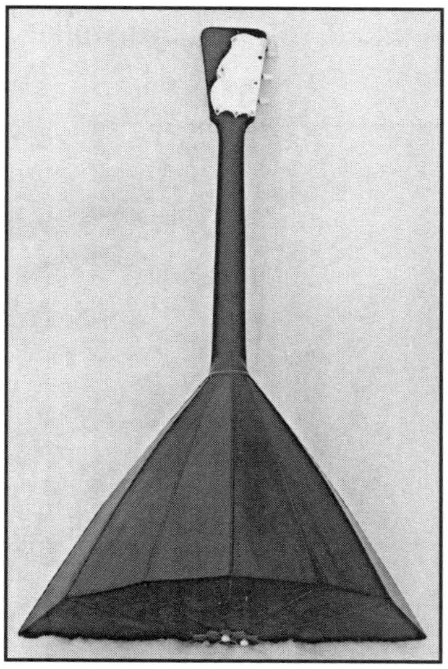

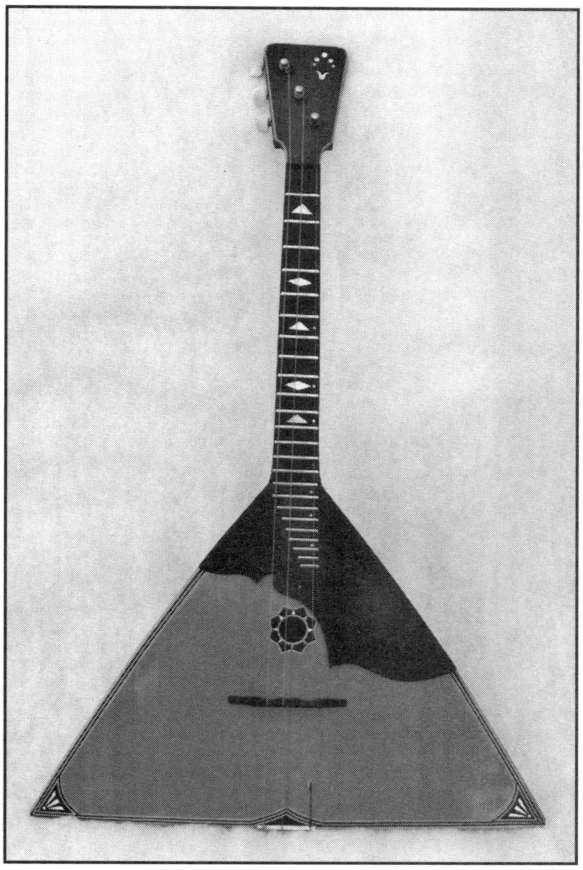

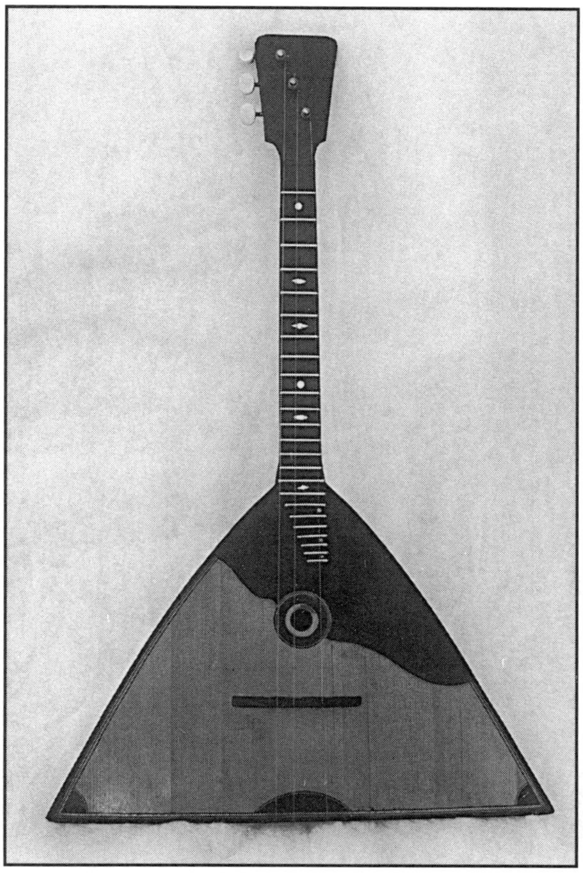

Prima of unknown maker from the turn of the century. The scratchplate is ebony veneer glued onto the soundboard.

Maple back, ebony neck and head.

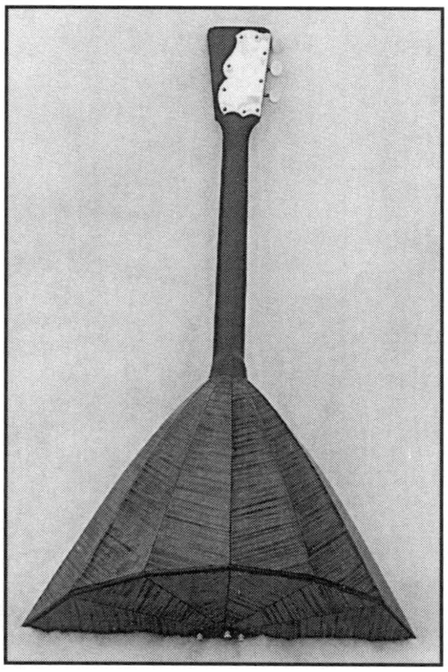

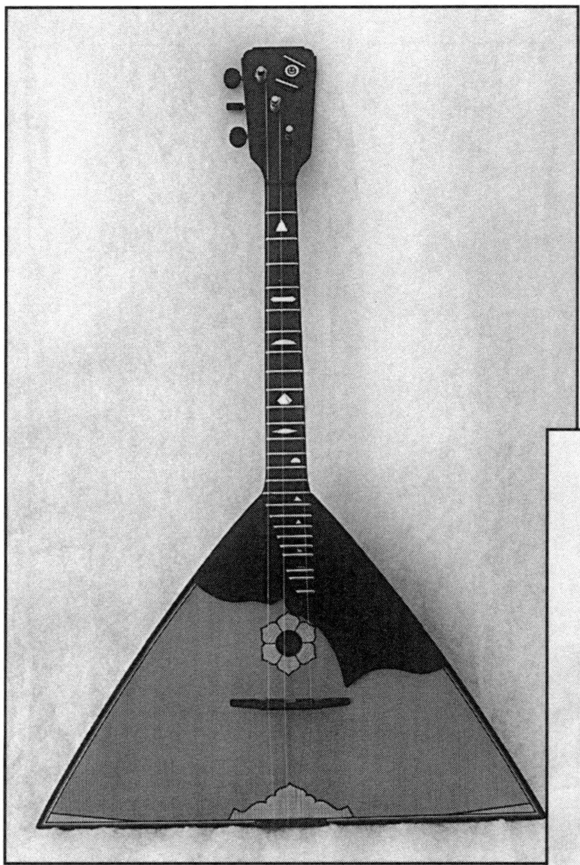

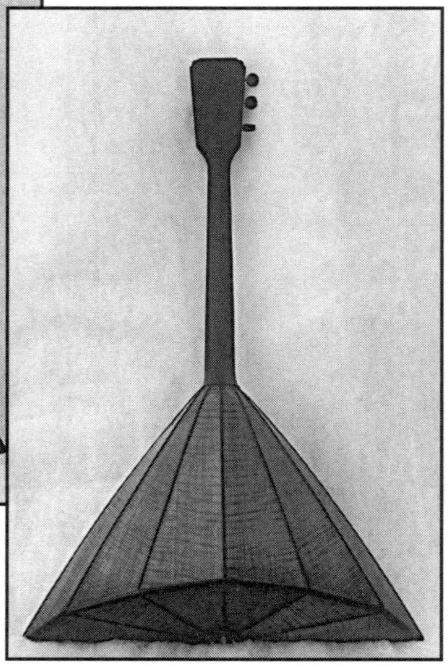

Modern prima balalaika by Andreas Gerth (Berlin), unique as a non-Russian maker of unsurpassed quality prima balalaikas. (See cover photo.) Made specifically for the author's hand, this instrument has an extremely comfortable, narrower-than-usual neck with rounded fingerboard, ebony head, neck, scratchplate, machine-head buttons and cover-plate. On the back, proud ribbing helps stop slipping during playing. Although very much a case of individual preference, a curved or rounded fingerboard makes use of the thumb much easier. This applies in an even greater degree to the alto balalaika with its wider neck. (It remains a mystery why Russian makers have so far failed to cotton on to this idea.)

Note the absence of the 26th fret, facilitating clear and accurate playing of the top 'C.' As an experiment the 23rd fret has also been removed on this instrument.

The inclusion of an extra mother-of-pearl dot on the 14th or 15th fret is a subject of individual preference.

Modern balalaika by Osipov (Moscow). Carefully-made, good-sounding instrument. An interesting feature is the recessed string-pins on the base of the instrument, preventing the strings or pins catching on clothing. (Balalaika players can sometimes be recognized not only by their unevenly-worn RH index finger nail, but by the snagged material on their RH inside trouser leg.)

It is a positive feature when these pins are spaced to correspond with the offset middle string. This prevents string pressure from pulling the bridge out of place on the soundboard. Despite beautiful workmanship and pretty inlays, including the soundhole, on this instrument the tuning pegs are typically of poor quality with aluminium buttons and cheap, brushed aluminium cover.

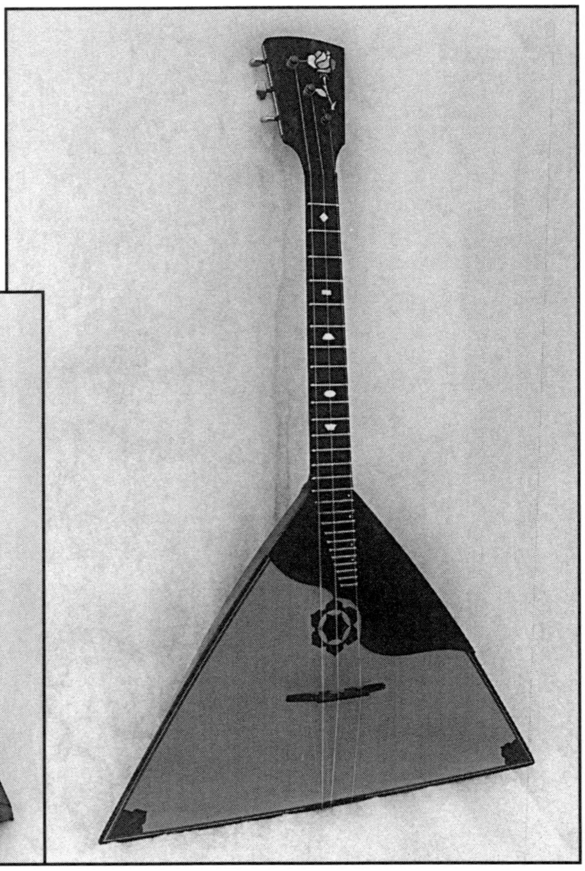

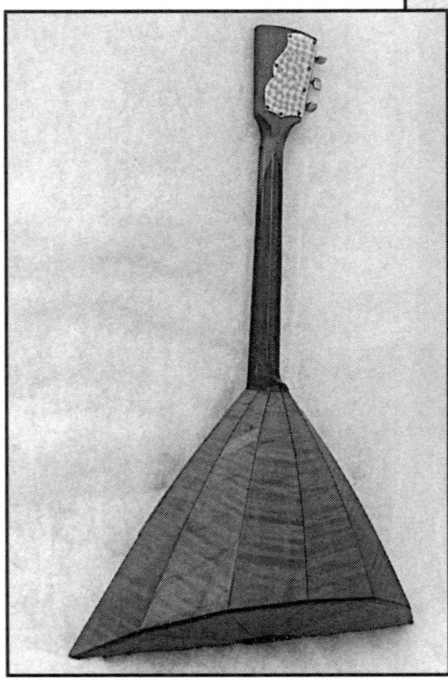

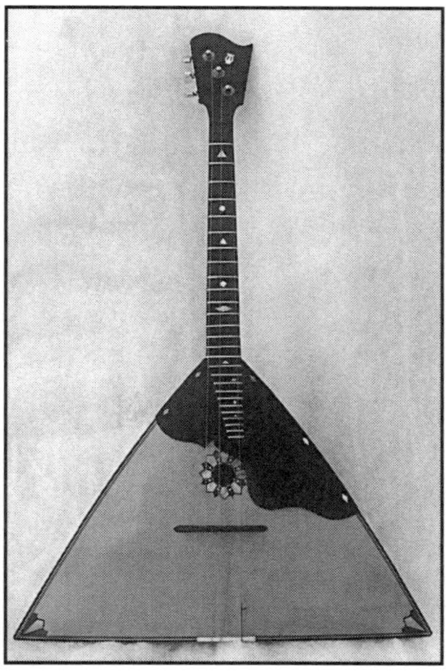

Ignatov (Moscow) - modern instrument with interesting scalloped back-ribs.
Having the scratchplate attached only in places, with spaces in-between, facilitates its easy removal when repairs or refretting are needed.

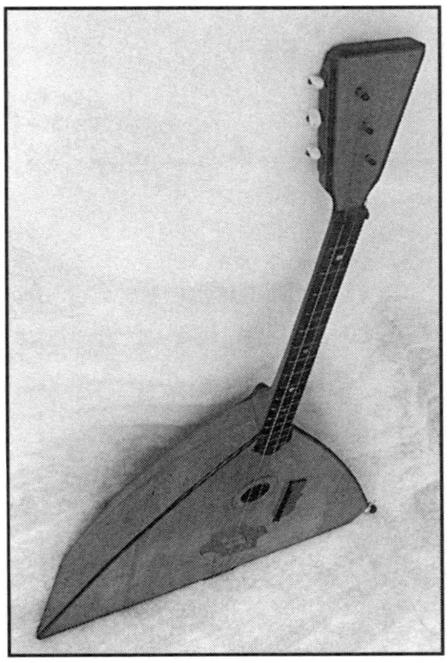

Bass Balalaika, Ziuzin (St. Petersburg) circa 1898. Seven-piece back, engraved silver machine-head cover. The spike is a later addition. Note the curious lipped finger-guard common to all basses and contrabasses of that period, but replaced by flush scratch-plates today. Inconvenient, if anything, when playing with a pick – one can only assume that back then it was traditional to hook the fingers over this lip and pluck the strings with the thumb.
An interesting fact is that this instrument, like its contemporaries of all orchestral sizes of balalaika and domra – including prima – were made slightly smaller than today's equivalents. People may have been physically smaller in those days, or maybe there has been a change for acoustic reasons. Whatever the case – some musicians, such as myself, find the old, smaller size of contrabass very convenient to travel with, when on the road.

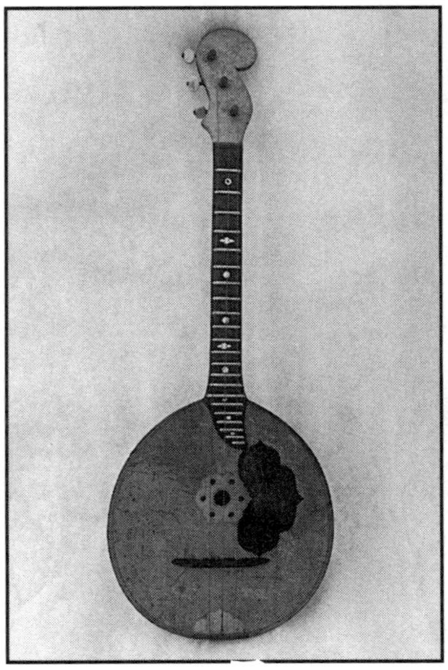

Ziuzin prima domra from the turn of the century. Noticeably smaller body than modern domras. Note the inlaid scratchplate, common for primas at that time.

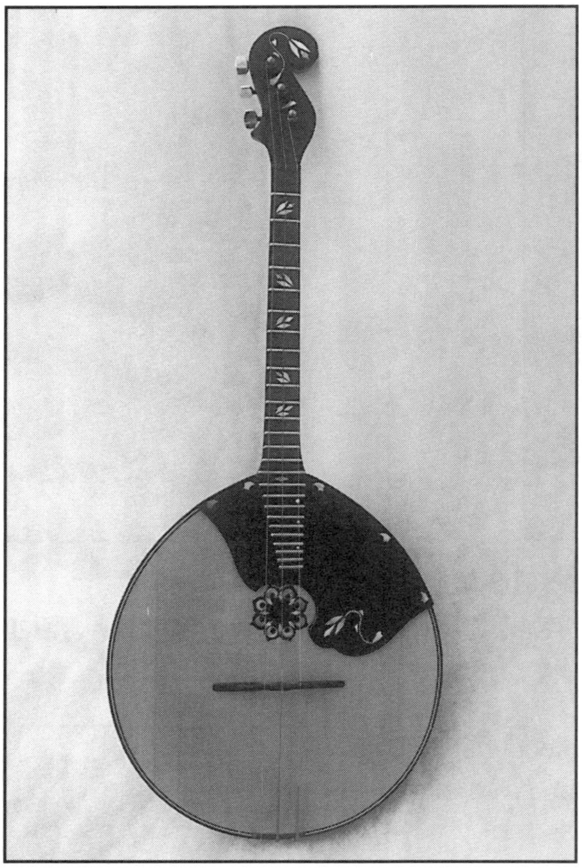

Modern domra by Serzhantov, Moscow. Today, three-string *primas* invariably have a raised, suspended scratchplate overhanging the soundboard; all larger sizes - an inlaid one (like on the Ziuzin shown previously).

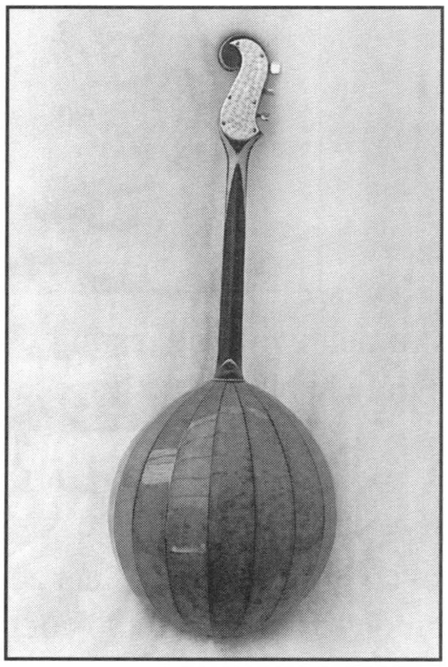

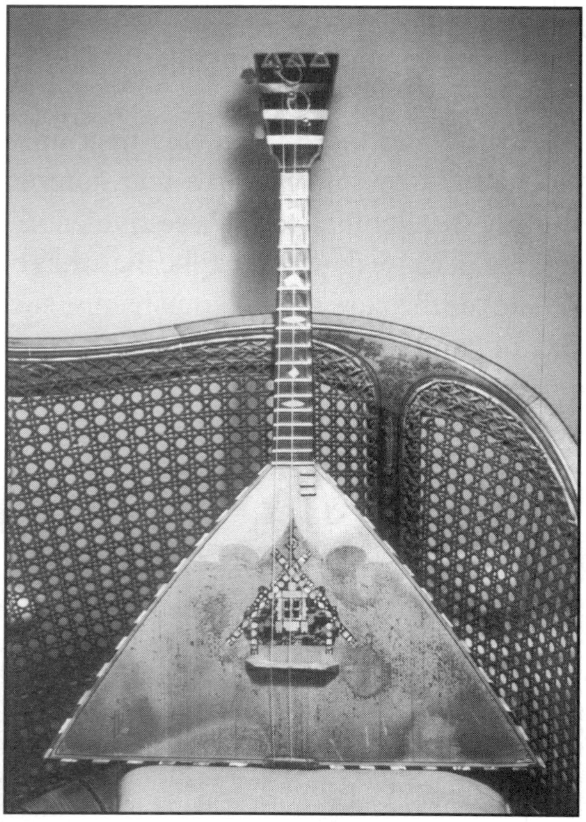

Pasyerbsky, circa 1890. Note the straight outline, shallow sound-box, birds-eye maple 7-piece back, symmetrical inlaid scratchplate. Attention to detailed decoration, mother-of-pearl embellishment and figure of wood, little house decoration of soundhole - popular at that time. Three extra frets are a later addition. The sound of this particular instrument was greatly improved by changing the maple two-footed banjo bridge subsequently for a longer, differently-shaped ebony one.

Bearing witness to the balalaika's heyday in the West - printed Tutors from circa 1911.

Pre-First World War articles and newspaper advertisements.

REPRINTED from the "DAILY MAIL," March 5th, 1910.
*INTERVIEW WITH CLIFFORD ESSEX.*

## How to Play the Balalaika.

THE GROWING POPULARITY OF THE RUSSIAN NATIONAL INSTRUMENT.

THE musical world has fallen in love with the balalaika. It is heard in drawing-rooms, on concert platforms, in Army mess-rooms; hostesses find that a balalaika band is a greater attraction at a musical "at home" than the most famous of tenors.

The balalaika is an instrument that can set your nerves tingling. It suggests moonlight and serenades. It can be plaintive as the violin and as maddeningly sweet as the harp.

Russia invented it; for hundreds of years it has been the national instrument of the peasants; its strings ring through the long, white winters; it is heard at every summer sunset. For generations voices have blended with its tones, and dancing feet have tripped to its music.

Prince Tchagadaeff, the leader of the Imperial Court orchestra, showed England the possibilities of the instrument last winter, when M. Andreeff's band performed in London; but it is only recently that amateurs have made the balalaika a fashionable craze. To-day half the world seems to be learning it.

The first attraction about the balalaika is the real beauty of its tone. It is soft, sweet, haunting. The second point in its favour is that it is the easiest of all musical instruments to learn. Mr. Clifford Essex, who taught hundreds of well-known folk to play the banjo when the fashion for that instrument was at its height, says that the balalaika is far easier to play. He has known pupils who have practically mastered it in eight lessons, and some who have been able to perform quite pleasingly after two weeks' practice.

The instruments, which are all imported from Russia, are simple yet handsome in appearance. Some of the most ornately decorated ones may cost as much as £25, but they can be obtained at as low a sum as thirty shillings.

The keyboard is something like that of a banjo, but is shorter, and there are only three strings. The first peculiarity that strikes the beginner is that two of the strings are tuned to the same note—E. The other string is tuned to A.

It is not played like the banjo, the mandoline, or the guitar, but in a manner quite peculiar to this one instrument.

The thumb of the left hand slides up and down the two E strings, while the other fingers are used for the higher notes on the A string.

The first finger of the right hand is passed rapidly and lightly over the three strings, and as it moves backwards and forwards a "tremolo" effect is produced. Occasionally all the four fingers of the right hand are swept across the strings to give the effect banjoists call the "rasp."

A hundred different effects seem possible with the balalaika. One of its beauties is the rather plaintive sliding note produced by the thumb and fingers gliding up and down the strings.

When played as a solo instrument it sounds well accompanied by a piano, but the possibilities of the balalaika cannot be properly understood till an entire band has been heard.

A balalaika orchestra is composed of almost any number of players, and the instruments they use are of different sizes, but all of the same pattern. There are prima, secunda, alt, bass, and contra-bass balalaikas.

Londoners will remember the haunting beauty of the Volga Boatman's Song, played by Prince Tchagadaeff's band. It is supposed to represent the droning chants sung by men as they carry heavy timber down to the boats. Like sailors who sing as they weigh the anchor, the Volga boatmen find that music helps them to keep time.

HAUNTING BEAUTY.

There seems every indication that the balalaika will soon be almost as well known in England as it is in its native Russia. Army men going abroad often take a few lessons before leaving England, knowing that in lonely stations music will be appreciated.

Mr. Rudyard Kipling says the banjo is "the war-drum of the English round the world."

The sweeter-toned balalaika seems to be taking its place.

Delicacy of Touch.

Mr. Clifford Essex begs to announce that his next

## Grand Concert

WILL TAKE PLACE AT

ST. JAMES'S HALL, GREAT PORTLAND STREET,

ON

Wednesday, June 8th,

AT 8 P.M.

In addition to the usual Banjo, Mandolin and Guitar features which have made all previous Concerts so successful, ***a great Novelty*** will be presented on this occasion by the appearance of a complete

## Balalaika Orchestra,

Conducted by Prince Tchagadaeff, of the Russian Imperial Court Balalaika Orchestra.

Popular Prices: Stalls, 5/-; Second Seats (Numbered and Reserved), 3/-; Unnumbered, 2/-; Admission, 1/-. Plan at 15A, Grafton Street, New Bond Street, W.

iv B.M.G. [September, 1913.

## Have You Realized

that either in solo or orchestral form, this instrument never fails to rouse an audience to the highest possible pitch of enthusiasm?

## Claim Your Share

of this success during the forthcoming season.

These instruments are of the finest quality procurable, and are

IMPORTED DIRECT FROM RUSSIA

BY THE

CLIFFORD ESSEX CO.

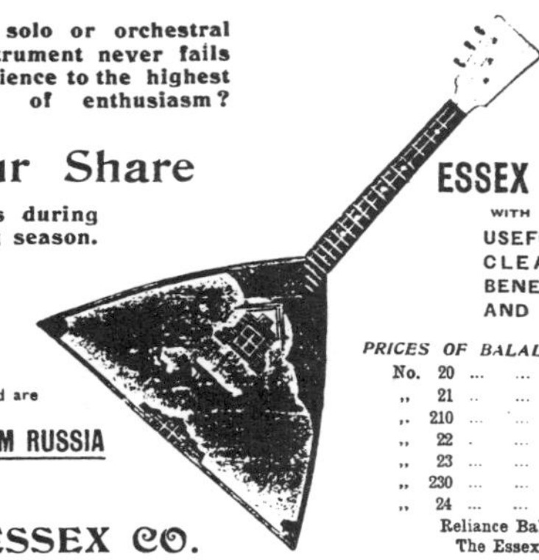

YOU CAN EASILY . .
INSTRUCT YOURSELF
BY MEANS OF THE .

ESSEX BALALAIKA TUTOR

WITH ITS . .
USEFUL ILLUSTRATIONS,
CLEAR LETTERPRESS,
BENEFICIAL EXERCISES,
AND EFFECTIVE SOLOS.

| *PRICES OF BALALAIKAS.* | £ | s. | d. |
|---|---|---|---|
| No. 20 | 1 | 10 | 0 |
| ,, 21 | 2 | 10 | 0 |
| ,, 210 | 3 | 10 | 0 |
| ,, 22 | 4 | 10 | 0 |
| ,, 23 | 5 | 10 | 0 |
| ,, 230 | 7 | 10 | 0 |
| ,, 24 | 10 | 10 | 0 |

Reliance Balalaika Cases, 13/- each.
The Essex Balalaika Tutor, 2 6.

## The London Coliseum, CHARING CROSS.

Managing Director ... ... ... OSWALD STOLL. Manager ... ... ... ... DUNDAS SLATER.

Twice Daily at 2.30 and 8 p.m.

By Special Permission of HIS IMPERIAL MAJESTY THE CZAR OF RUSSIA.
RETURN VISIT OF THE RUSSIAN IMPERIAL COURT ORCHESTRA.

W. W. ANDREEF'S (The)

# RUSSIAN BALALAIKA COURT ORCHESTRA.

W. W. ANDREEF'S Balalaika Orchestra is maintained and controlled by the Crown, and almost every member has been the recipient of Russian or Foreign Decorations, whilst each Instrument has been Specially Designed and Constructed by the leader, resulting in an ensemble which is both Unique and Original.

THERE EXISTS NO OTHER NATIONAL ORCHESTRA OF A SIMILAR CHARACTER.

APPEARED BY ROYAL COMMAND—First at WINDSOR, Nov. 20th, 1909; Second at SANDRINGHAM, Dec. 1st, 1909.

IN ADDITION A POWERFUL VARIETY COMPANY.

# Repertoire Section

## "BAA-BAA BLACK SHEEP" - *English Nursery Rhyme*

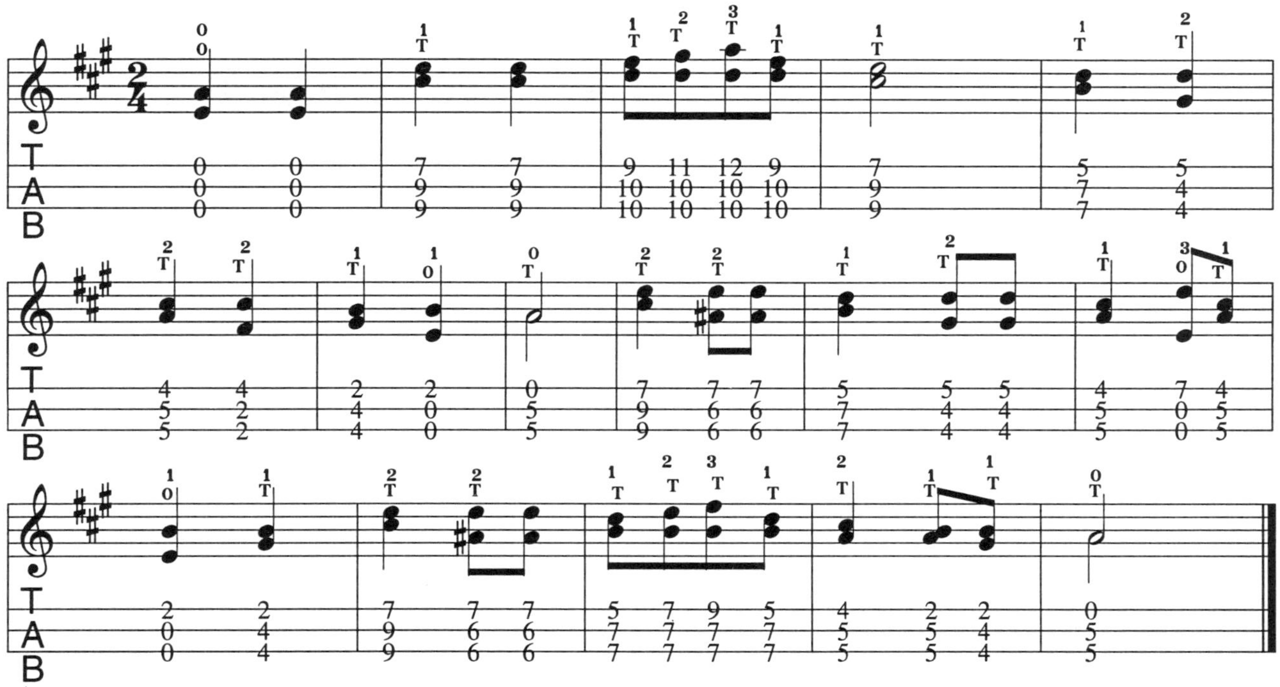


## "THE SLENDER ROWAN TREE" - *Russian Folk Song*

(Tonkaya Ryabina)

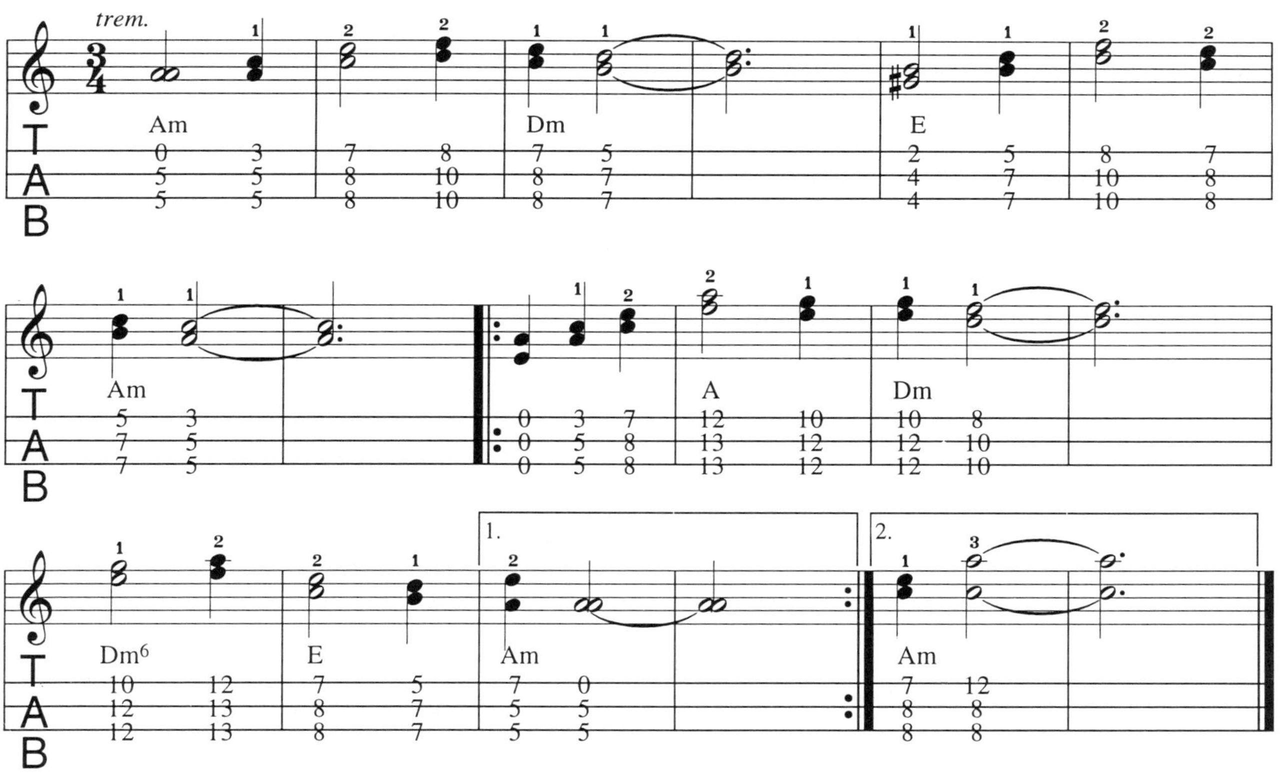

## "GOD SAVE THE CZAR"

Anthem of Imperial Russia

A. Lvov
arr.: B. Ekkel

## "IN THE FIELD A BIRCH TREE STOOD" - *Russian Folk Song*

(Vo polye beryozka stoyala)

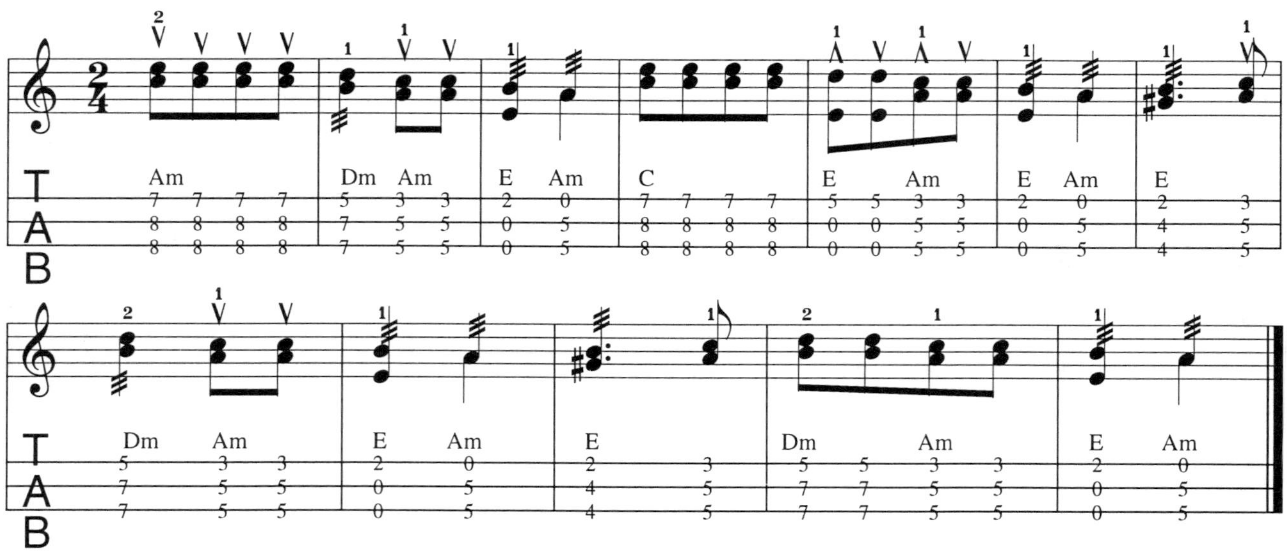

## "THE URAL ROWAN TREE"

(Uralskaya ryabinushka)

Ye. Rodygin

## "IT'S NOT THE WIND THAT BENDS THE BRANCH" - *Russian Folk Song*
(To nie veter vetku klonit)

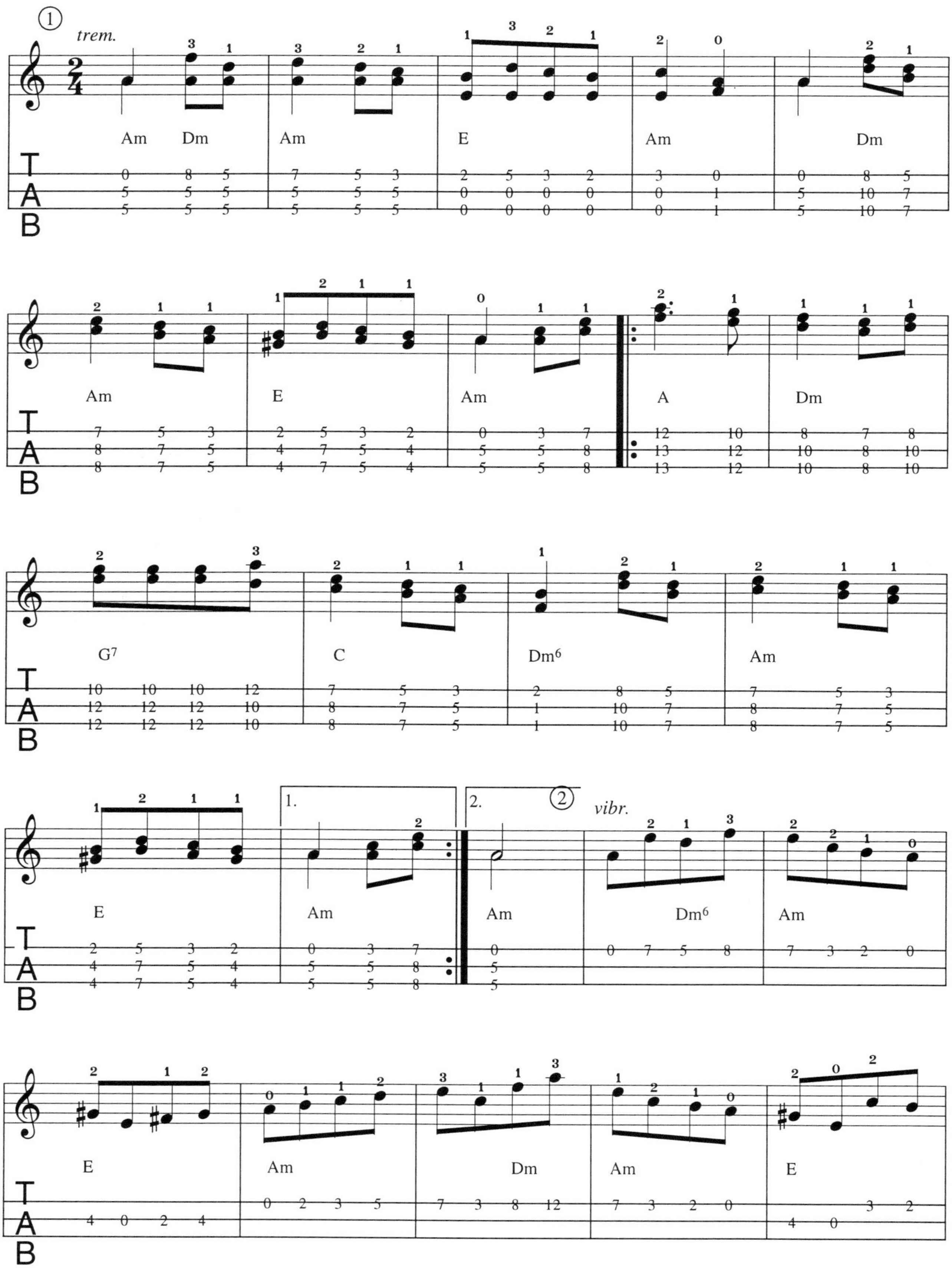

Am F A Dm G C
Dm6 Am E Am Am
1. 2.
trem.
Am Dm6 Am E Am Dm6
Am E Am F A
Dm G7 C Dm6
Am E Am Am
1. 2.
TAB

## "DANCE, DANCE" - *Slovak Melody*
(Tancuj, tancuj)

## "VARYAG" - *Russian Folk Song*

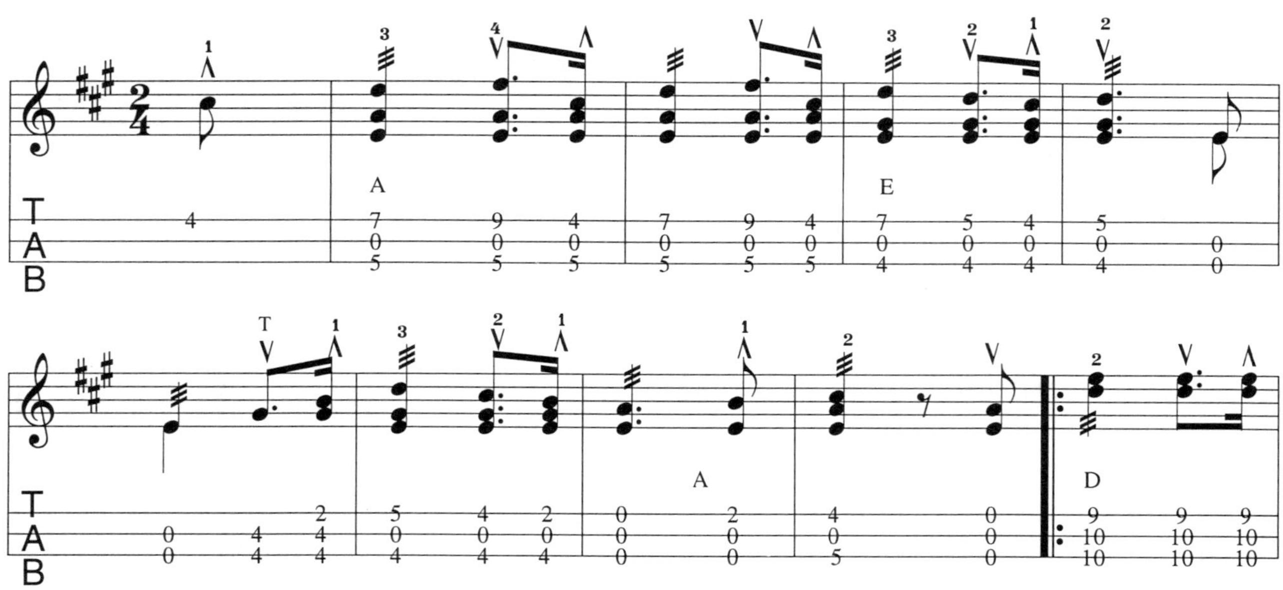

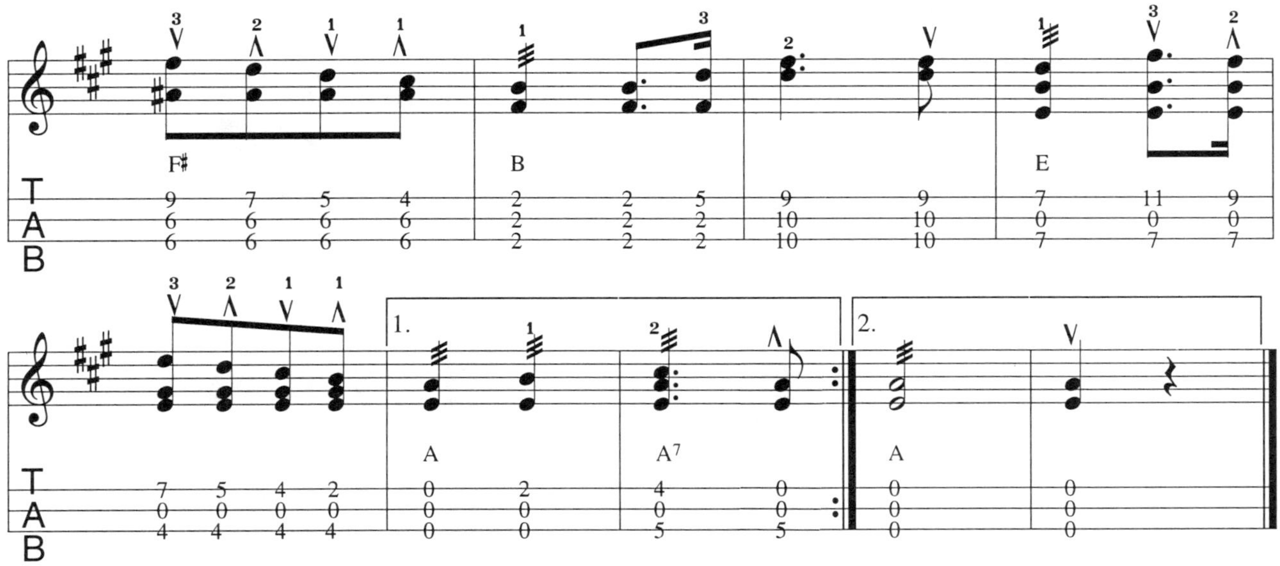


## "DO NOT SCOLD ME" - *Russian Folk Song*

(Nie brani menya, rodnaya)

arr.: Bibs Ekkel

# "I SHALL GO DOWN TO THE RIVER" - *Russian Folk Song*

(Vyidu ya na rechen'ku)

## "I LOVED YOU" - *Russian Romance*
(Ya vas lubil)

Count Sheremyetev
arr.: B. Ekkel

## "GOIN' HOME"

## "I WAS IN THE GARDEN" - *Russian Folk Song*
(Ya v sadochke byla)

## "THE POST TROIKA HASTENS" - *Russian Folk Song*
(Vot mchitsya troika pochtovaya)

## "MOONSHINE" - *Russian Folk Song*

(Probably the most widely-played of balalaika melodies)

arr.: B. Ekkel

E
A
E
A
D
A
D
A
E
A
E
A

p
D
A
D
A
E
A
E
A
mf
D
A
D
A

f
E
A
A
E
p
D
A7
D
A
f
E
A
E
A

D
A
D
A
E
A
E
A
1.
2.
D
A7
D
T T T T
A
TAB

p
E
A
E
A
1.
2.
f
D
A
D
A
E
A
F♯
Bm
Dm6
E
A
gliss.
ff

# "AKH, NASTASYA"

*Variations on a Russian Melody*

A. Dobrokhotoff

Dm
E
Am
Am
Dm
E
Am
Am
Dm
E
Am
Am
Dm
E
Am
Am

## "UNDER THE APPLE TREE" - *Russian Folk Melody*

(Kak pod yablonkoy)

arr.: B. Ekkel

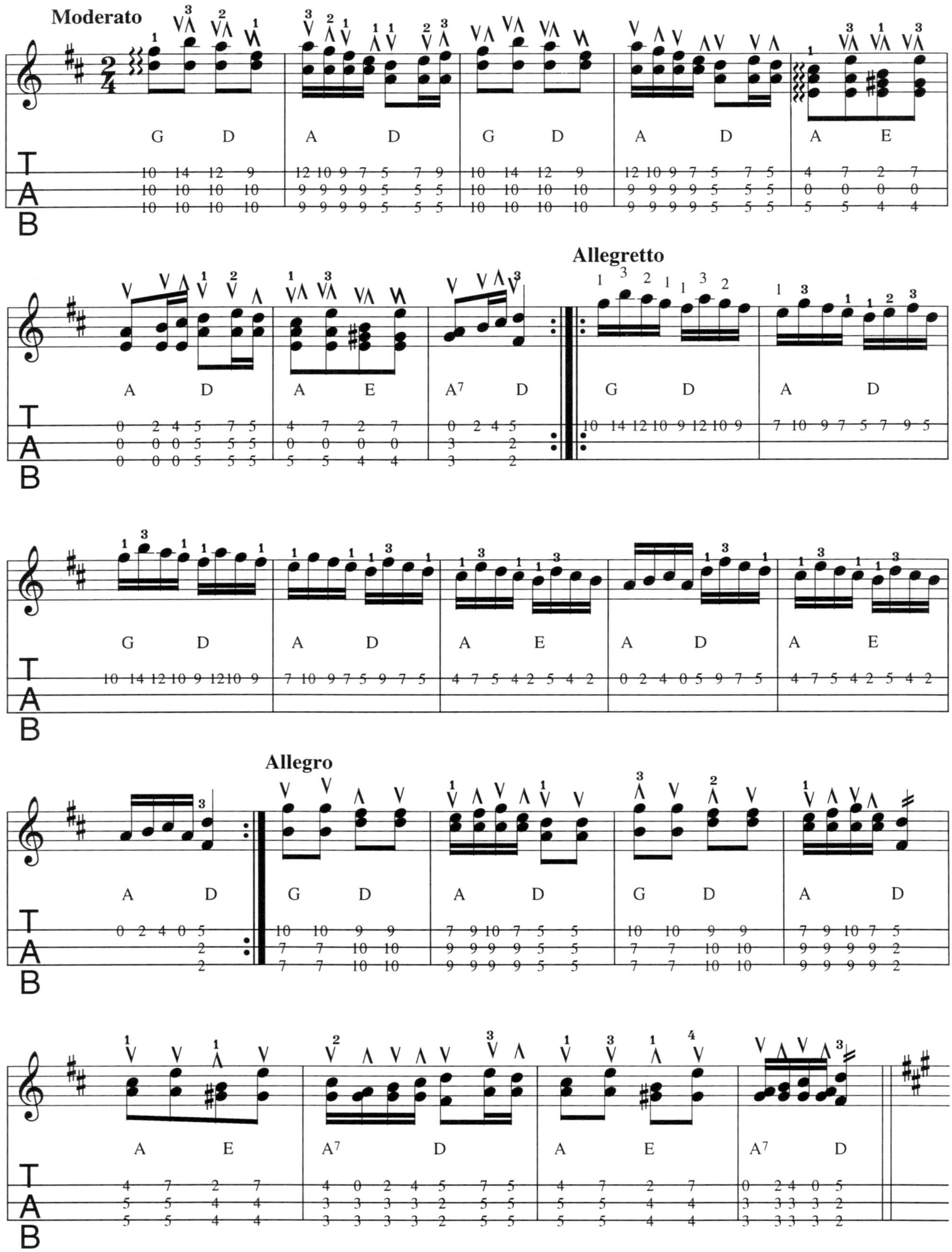

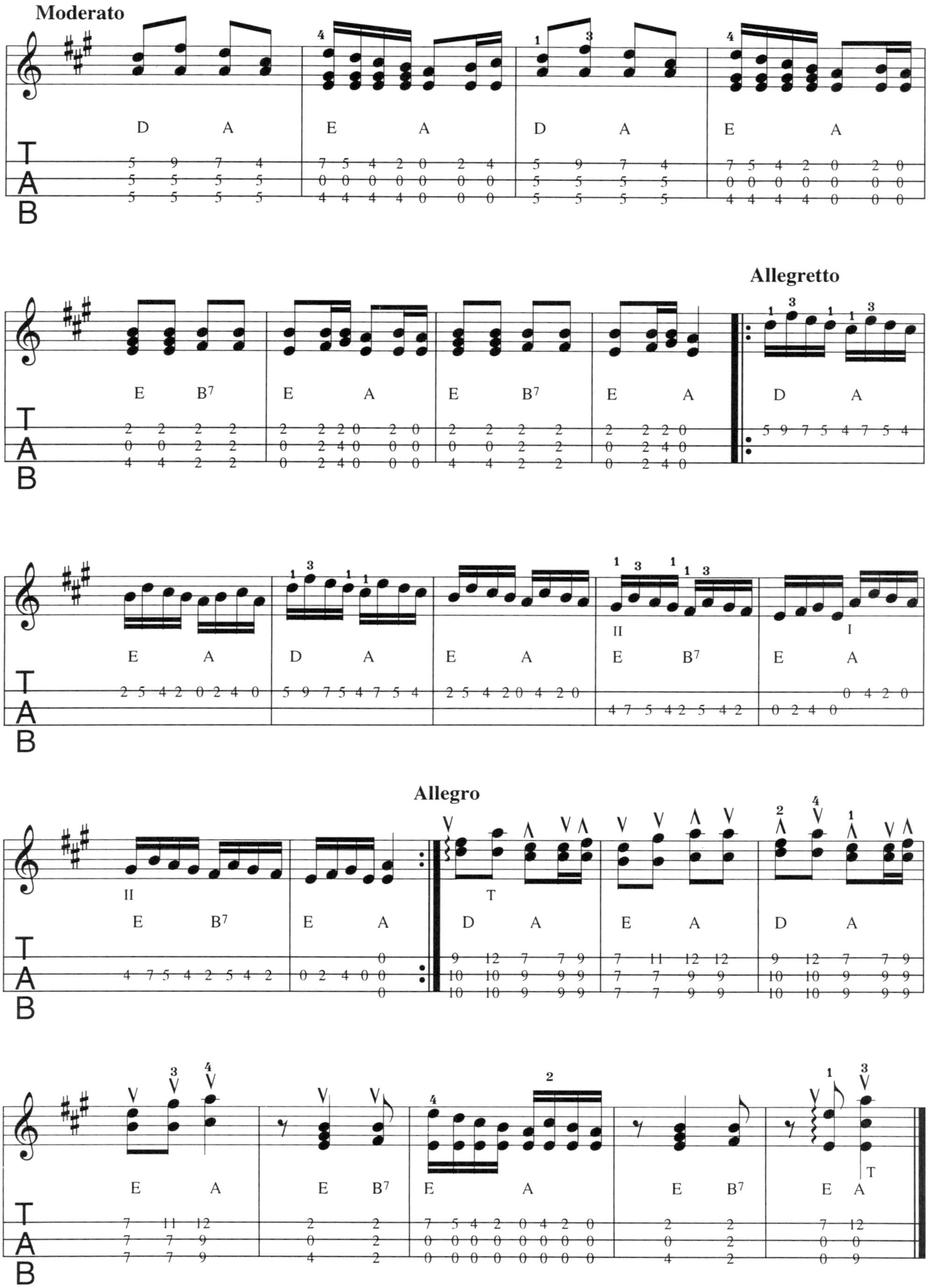
Moderato
D A E A D A E A
E B7 E A E B7 E A
Allegretto
D A
E A D A E A E B7 E A
E B7 E A
Allegro
D A E A D A
E A E B7 E A E B7 E A

# "POLOSYNKA" - *Russian Folk Song*

arr.: P. Manich/B. Ekkel

A Dm A Dm A7 Dm6 Am E Am Dm6
Am E Am A Dm A Dm A Dm
A7 Dm Am E Am Dm Am E
Am A Dm A7 Dm A Dm
A Dm Am E7 Am F Am E7 Am

## "GO HOME YOU GOSSIPS" - *Russian Folk Melody*

(Ay, vsye kumushki domoy)

Boris Troyanovsky*

(* Boris Sergeyevich Troyanovsky - one of the earliest balalaika virtuosi, considered the founder of the modern school of balalaika technique.)

## "DARK BROWED, DARK EYED LAD" - *Russian Folk Song*

(Chernobrovyi, chernookii)

arr.: B. Ekkel

## "TWO GUITARS" - *Russian Gypsy Song*
(Dvie gitary)

arr.: B. Ekkel

Gm Dm A7 Dm
p Gm Dm A Dm
Gm Dm A Dm
f Gm Dm A7 Dm
Gm Dm A Dm
Moderato
vibr
Dm Am E Am
Dm Am E Am
TAB

E
Am
E
Am
A
Dm
Am
accelerando
E
Am
Dm
II
Am
E7
Am
Dm
Am
E
Am
Dm
Am
E
Am
Dm
Am
E
Am
TAB

Dm Am II E Am
TAB
Dm Am E Am
TAB
Dm Am E7 Am A Dm
TAB
Am E Am Dm
TAB
Am E Am Dm Am
TAB
E Am Dm Am
TAB
E Am Dm E Am
TAB

# "KATIUSHA" - *Popular Russian Song*

M. Blanter/ arr.: B. Ekkel

guit.pizz.
guit.pizz.

vibr.
Am
E
Am
G7
C
F
C
A
Dm
Am
Dm
Am
E
Am
C
F
C
A
Dm
Am
Dm
Am
E
Am
TAB

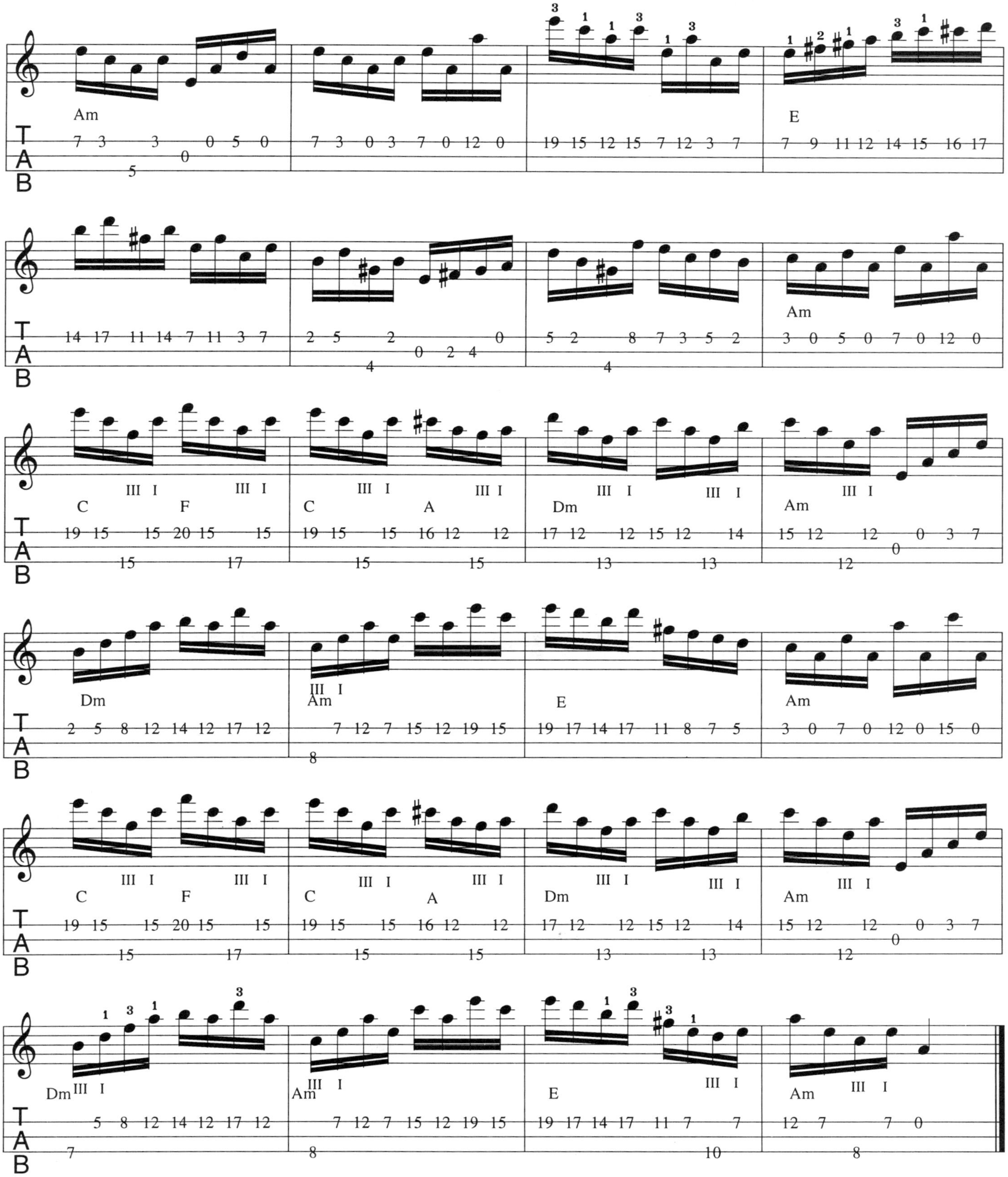
Am
E
Am
C F
C A
Dm
Am
Dm
Am
E
Am
C F
C A
Dm
Am
Dm
Am
E
Am

# "FOR CZAR, MOTHERLAND AND FAITH"

(Veshchii Oleg) - *Czarist March*

## "A COSSACK CROSSED THE DANUBE" - *Ukrainian Folk Song*

(Yikhav kozak za Dunai)

arr.: B. Ekkel

III
C
G
E
Am
E
Am
II
Am
E
Am
E
Am
G7
C
G
E
Am
E
Am

Dm
A
Dm
A
Dm C7
F
C
A7
Dm
B♭ E
A
Dm
Dm
A
Dm
A
Dm C

F III I C III I A7
Dm A Dm
Dm A
Dm A Dm C7
F C A7
Dm A Dm

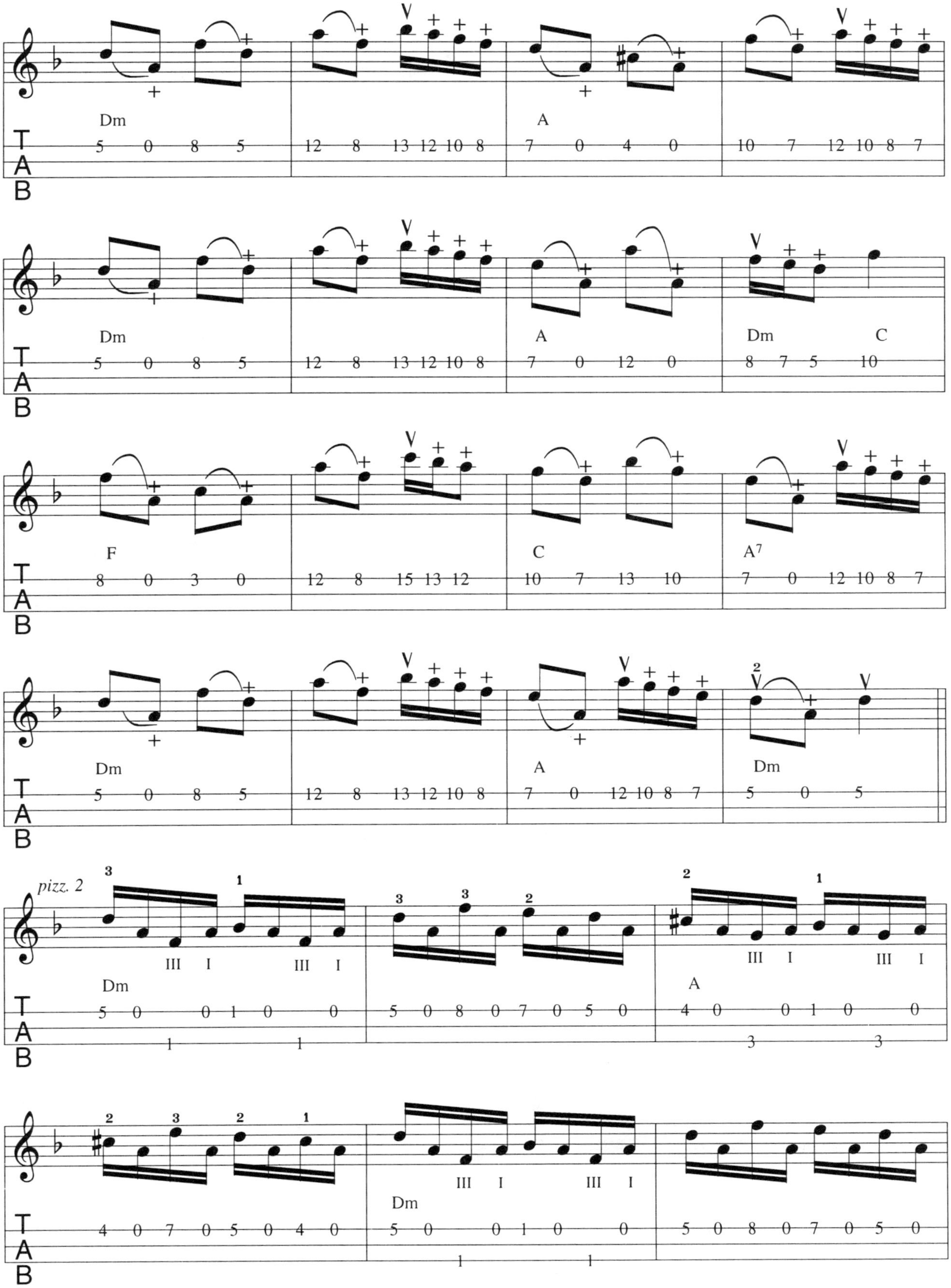
Dm
A
Dm
A
Dm C
F
C
A7
Dm
A
Dm
pizz. 2
Dm
A
Dm

A
Dm
F
III I
C
A
Dm
A
Dm
Dm
simile
A
TAB

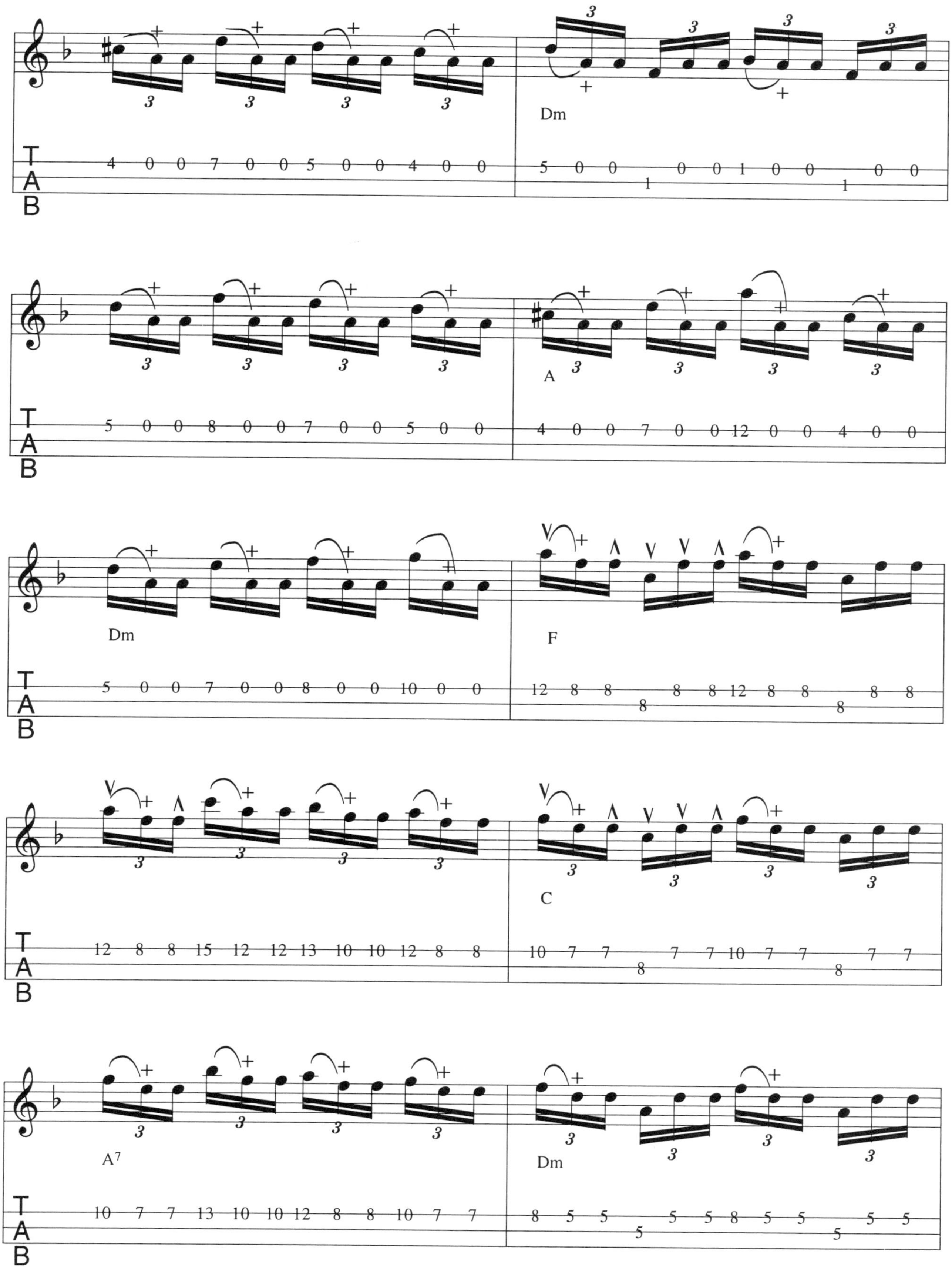
TAB
Dm
TAB
A
TAB
Dm
F
TAB
C
TAB
A7
Dm
TAB

A
Dm
Dm Dm+5
Dm6
A
A7
B♭
E
A7
Dm C
F
G7
C
A7
rit.
Dm Dm+5
G E
A
Dm

## "LEAF FROM AN ALBUM"

(Listok iz alboma)

M. I. Glinka
arr.: Bibs Ekkel

3
3
6

## "DAYDREAMS" - *for Balalaika Orchestra*
(Gryozy)

V. V. Andreyev/ arr.: B. Ekkel

18
24

30
mf
p
36
f

2
42
mp
mp
mp
2
trem.
mp
mp
mp
mp
mp
48

54
60

66
f
FINE
3
72

78
84
rit.
rit.
rit.
rit.
rit.
rit.

90
f
p
96

1.
2.
102
f
Dal Segno al Fine
Dal Segno al Fine